PRAISE FO...
KRISTEN DALTON WOLFE AND

THE SPARKLE EFFECT

"You have an extraordinarily unique brand of beautiful with which God wants to paint this world. Kristen shows us how to believe it, embrace it, and live it with the biblical understanding of who we are created to be." —Lysa TerKeurst, *New York Times* bestselling author and president of Proverbs 31 Ministries

"I love Kristen's mission and her coming alongside women to do life well. In this book, she gives some great areas for focus to get there, including setting standards and boundaries as a confident, empowered woman of God." —Dr. Henry Cloud, psychologist and *New York Times* bestselling author

"This book is a magical read that conveys the truth of who you are, what you deserve, and what you have access to as God's daughter in a new, refreshing way. You'll feel like you're diving into real talk with real stories and real guidance from a gentle yet strong sister." —Bianca Juarez Olthoff, freedom fighter, speaker, and bestselling author

"Kristen is such a delightful woman and has a genuine desire to help young women fulfill their God-given purpose! Her words are encouraging and honest, and will be a great help.... You will feel like you have spent time with a friend!"
—Holly Wagner, pastor at Oasis Church, author of *GodChicks* and *Find Your Brave*, and founder of the She Rises conference

"A delightful guide on how to overcome! Kristen addresses the core struggles and secret heart pains of a woman...and coaching points on how to be set free so you can finally shine again."

—Rosie Rivera, author and TV personality

"THE SPARKLE EFFECT is a must read for every woman. Whether you are personally struggling with self-worth or on the journey to embrace all God has for you, this book will be your guide." —Tammy Hotsenpiller, founder and president of Women of Influence

"With this book, not only will you learn to love yourself and learn how to sparkle, but you will know just how loved you are by our heavenly father." —Greer Grammer, actress on MTV's *Awkward* and ABC's *The Middle*

"As an actor who has played a queen onscreen, Kristen's book reminded me we are all royalty in real life. Kristen, whom I deeply admire, empowers me to walk in the fullness of that identity."

—Rachel Skarsten, Queen Elizabeth on CW's *Reign*

"An inspiring guide to build up your heart to withstand criticism and judgment, and an unfaltering ability to keep your chin up...after reading this book you'll surely get your shine on!"

—Alyssa Quilala, author, pastor, actress, and model

"Kristen...uses her personal experience along with scripture to encourage her audience to give their hearts wholly to their creator. And beyond encouraging her readers, she gives us tangible examples of what it means and how to live life with the 'Sparkle Effect.'"

—Savvy Shields, Miss America 2017

"Kristen has an undeniable, God-given gift of wisdom and inspiring others.... [Her] message in this book is absolutely necessary in these times of self-doubt and fear."

—Leven Rambin, Glimmer on *The Hunger Games*

"In a world where so many struggle with their identity and worth, Kristen's book offers keys to being a beautiful reflection of God's attributes inside and out. A must-read for every young lady and woman who questions her value."

—Michelle McKinney Hammond, bestselling author of *The Power of Being a Woman,* and Emmy Award–winning TV host

"Kristen's wisdom is such a gift. Far too often, we have been taught to belittle ourselves and our power. In THE SPARKLE EFFECT, Kristen addresses every aspect of our heavenly identity. She tackles tough issues, overlooked issues, and, most important, issues of the heart. This book shares the necessary tools and truths that can help women of all ages begin to uncover who God made them to be!"

—Spencer Locke, Jane on *Tarzan*

"Kristen's sparkling big-sister heart for women shines through in this beautifully honest, grounded, and poignant book. She lets us into her life, to her personal journey toward wholeness, with stories and encouragements that are heartfelt and rooted in the Word. As you read, you're sure to be drawn closer to the heart of Jesus, and empowered to become the person you were created to be."

—Amanda Jane Cooper, Glinda on *Wicked* on Broadway

"A very uplifting and empowering read.... I felt inspired and motivated to attack my day with much more confidence."

—Meagan Tandy, CEO of the Meagan Tandy Foundation and Empire Girls

"I really respect Kristen's way of filtering life through the wisdom she's gathered from her faith. Knowing her personally, I can say that she really does practice what she preaches, and you can see that fruit in her life. This book is her sharing her secrets with the world."

—Caitlin Crosby Benward, founder and CEO of The Giving Keys

THE

Sparkle

EFFECT

*Step into the Radiance of
Your True Identity*

KRISTEN DALTON WOLFE

with a Foreword by
Sheri Rose Shepherd

New York   Nashville

FaithWords
Hachette Book Group
1290 Avenue of the Americas, New York, NY 10104
faithwords.com
twitter.com/faithwords

First Edition: October 2018

FaithWords is a division of Hachette Book Group, Inc. The FaithWords name and logo are trademarks of Hachette Book Group, Inc.

The publisher is not responsible for websites (or their content) that are not owned by the publisher.

The Hachette Speakers Bureau provides a wide range of authors for speaking events. To find out more, go to www.hachettespeakersbureau.com or call (866) 376-6591.

Library of Congress Cataloging-in-Publication Data has been applied for.

ISBNs: 978-1-5460-3176-5 (paperback), 978-1-5460-2717-1 (ebook)

Printed in the United States of America

LSC-C

10 9 8 7 6 5 4 3 2 1

This book is dedicated to my mother, Jeannine, who instilled in me a love for Jesus and a reverence for the Lord since I was a young girl. She has shown me what it looks like to sparkle in the midst of life's hardships and pain. I wouldn't be who I am today without her sacrificial love, prayers, and guidance. Thank you, Mama, for being the generous, wise, resilient, good-humored woman you are. You deserve all the honor in the world.

Contents

Foreword

Dear friend:

I'm proud of you for having the bravery to pick up this book. *The Sparkle Effect* sounds so pretty and easy and twirly, but the art of having it and keeping it is not. As a young girl, I believed "sparkling" was for other girls... girls who were tall, thin, talented, smart, and those who came from wealthy families and had all the trendy clothes, gadgets, and boyfriends. The notion of sparkling was definitely not for me. I was overweight, depressed, dyslexic, and bullied. Not even my teachers believed in me. One of them told me I'd never go anywhere in life because of my reading impairment. If only I'd known Kristen.

Back then, I would have given anything to curl up in my bed to read the raw and powerful secrets and stories Kristen shares in this book. It could have saved me a long journey of mistakes, self-hatred, an eating disorder, believing lies about myself, and even a suicide attempt. I truly struggled. Then when I won the titles of Miss USA and Mrs. America, I thought that surely they would soothe all my self-doubt, insecurities, and inner pain. I thought they would give me confidence and make me feel beautiful. But I was terribly mistaken. They left me emptier and more lost than before. Titles and accolades only breed more emptiness when they aren't driven by wholeness.

But could I be whole? Can anyone sparkle? Or is that just reserved for certain, special people God seems to love more?

It took me many years, in which I experienced heartbreaks that shattered me into pieces, before I realized my worth. I don't want you to have to hit rock bottom to finally realize that you can sparkle, too, regardless of your circumstances.

That's what I remembered when I met Kristen: that no matter what, I can sparkle.

One day, I received an interview request from Kristen Dalton Wolfe for her show on Trinity Broadcasting Network. Unbeknownst to her, I had been going through one of the darkest times in my life.

I canceled and rescheduled my interview with Kristen a few times. She was patient with me, and when I finally met her in January 2017, I immediately knew why God wanted us to meet. I came alive in our interview. She drew out the gold in me and made me feel on fire again.

As we talked, I remembered that I had watched her compete the year she won Miss USA. When the camera panned to her face during the Miss USA telecast, I knew she was a woman of faith. She had a light about her and a sparkle in her eyes. I actually prayed throughout the competition night that she would win. And thank God she did or I might not have gotten my fight back. Kristen said she has looked up to me as an author and role model for a long time, but the day we met, I told her that I was adopting her as my spiritual daughter. We began texting regularly after our first meeting. One day soon after, she wrote me about a vision God had given her for a women's conference. She told me she wanted me to speak with her. I had barely begun to pray about it before God responded with a resounding YES.

What Kristen didn't know was I was about to ask her to speak with me.

My standard is very high regarding the character of those whom I minister beside. The reason I felt confident aligning myself with Kristen is her pure heart. Her motives are pure. She is completely devoted to her walk with God and has no interest in settling, compromising her values, or selling out for fame. She isn't driven by anything other than sharing God's heart for other women. She has a fire in her soul to see women experience a personal revelation of their royal identity, to be free and confident in the Lord, and to boldly live out their calling. Many people set out to do this, but few have the character and persistence to match the task. Kristen has it; that's why I'm glad you're reading this book.

Kristen became a Miss USA because of the sparkle everyone saw in her eyes that night. Now, she is stewarding the platform God gave her to teach women like you how to unveil their sparkle, too. It starts on the inside. You don't have to live with depression, self-doubt, shame, insecurity, or the constant urge to people-please anymore. You get to be the girl who knows herself, who loves the skin she is in, who commands respect, and who unapologetically lives out her purpose—no matter who hurts her or what obstacles she encounters.

This book is like no other I've read. No one has ever defined what it takes to have the "it factor" the way Kristen does. But this book is so much more than that. If you read it with an open heart, you will close these pages having become closer to the woman God made you to be: strong, bold, focused, determined, gentle, secure, dazzling, fervent, gracious, faithful, and irresistibly you.

Precious girl, let these pages take you on a journey to discover the sparkle within you and to ultimately let it shine.

Sheri Rose Shepherd

Letter from Kristen

Dear Queen:

Writing this book is a dream come true. For a long time, I've had a heart for helping young women step into their true identity. I want to take you on a journey that will release a radiance that stands out beyond beauty. You will discover that it's not always the qualities on the outside that make a girl stand out on her quest to fulfill her dream. Having the Sparkle Effect isn't about having the best résumé, clothes, hair, body, skin, money, fans, followers, family, or circumstances. Having the Sparkle Effect means that you emanate the special *it factor* when you've experienced Jesus as the identity transformer. Throughout this book, I will explain what this means, how I learned to have the Sparkle Effect that helped me achieve my dreams, and how you can, too.

One Sunday, I was in worship at church. My eyes were closed as I soaked in the thick, sweet presence of God. My mind drifted to an image of me as a thirteen-year-old girl. I had short hair and was sitting at the fireplace in our family living room. My eyes were sad. There was a heaviness over me. As I recalled how I felt back then, tears started rolling down my cheeks and I grieved for that young girl. A young girl who felt alone, rejected, and depressed, yet who was so good at smiling and acting happy. I hurt for the girl who was unsure where she fit into the world, while trying to convince the world she was sure. My heart also broke for any girl who ever feels this way.

Then, in a vision, God showed me who He is and who I really am.

I saw Jesus crown me and suddenly my sadness was lifted and everything burst into color, brilliance, and sparkle. The cloud looming over me was eradicated by light. My eyes became bright, clear, and joyful. It was as if the fairy godmother from *Cinderella* had touched me with her wand and transformed my rags into a glittering gown.

As I saw this vision, tears fell down my face. My life flashed before my eyes, like a movie reel, clearly revealing how God had transformed me. The moment I let Him crown me, my life changed. He wants to crown you, too.

Jesus is an identity transformer. He crowns us with renewal, radiance, favor, blessings, and tender loving mercies. When we know who we are and confidently walk in our Kingdom inheritance, a sparkle emerges. It's a sparkle that's undeniably magnetic, and a sparkle that can change the world around you for good.

God has beautiful dreams for your life. You may feel trapped, lifeless, hopeless, or clueless right now. You don't have to stay that way anymore. As I take you through this journey, let's forget all the ways the world has taught you to stand out or succeed. Let's unmask who you were created to be. Let's transform your heart and ignite the radiance in your eyes. Let's unveil what it really takes to have the Sparkle Effect.

On that day the LORD their God will rescue his people, just as a shepherd rescues his sheep. They will sparkle in his land like jewels in a crown. (Zechariah 9:16 NLT)

Love,
Kristen

The Sparkle Effect

I don't remember a lot about the moment I was crowned Miss USA 2009. I stood in the top five after my final questions were complete. The runner-up placements were being called one by one. The stakes were the highest they had ever been in my life. Adrenaline was pumping through my body as I waited to hear if I was moving to New York City the next day or going back home. This was the moment I had dreamed of since I was a little girl. The reality of my dream was about to be determined, after a commercial break. A surreal elation swirled around me, I let out a scream, and my hands flew over my face! I couldn't believe it, but I *could* totally believe it. I had envisioned it so many times, it was seared into my subconscious mind.

I was so excited to meet head judge Shandi Finnessey after the competition. She was Miss USA 2004 and one of my role models. Earlier in the night, I had been so giddy when I saw her looking up at me from the judges panel.

How am I going to stay composed in the final question with her sitting there? I wondered.

When Shandi and I met afterward, she congratulated me and I thanked her. Then she told me something I will always remember. She said, "After the top fifteen contestants were announced, all of the judges leaned in and asked me, 'Every girl here is beautiful. How do we know who to choose?'"

"You will see it in one girl—the one who sparkles," she answered. "You will see it in her eyes and smile."

After the commercial break, they all leaned back in and said, "We see her. We see the girl who sparkles."

She looked at me intently and said, "That girl was you."

In that moment I was so thankful and humbled, but it wasn't until later that I would realize the magnitude of her statement.

Since I was three years old, my dream was to become Miss USA. My mother is a former Miss North Carolina USA, and we watched the Miss America and the Miss USA pageants every year with my sisters. It was like a holiday at our house. My mama would curl our hair in sponge rollers, we'd eat popcorn with Milk Duds and sip orange juice out of a thermos we all shared.

The winning moment got me every time. I remember sitting there in my red-and-white-striped nightgown, eyes wide and my heart palpitating when the final two women held hands on that stage. My sisters and I held hands in hopes that our favorite girl won. But when they announced the winner, it didn't matter who it was. Her reaction emanated redemption of past rejection, hard work that had paid off, and adversities she had overcome. Even as a little girl, I cried during the crowning moment. It was as if I could feel everything the new Miss USA was feeling. I looked up to her and I wanted to inspire a little girl like me one day as well.

Growing up, I had a quiet, inner knowing that becoming Miss USA was my destiny. It inspired decisions I made and helped me cope with whatever I was facing.

For example, when I was getting my braces painfully tightened in the orthodontist's chair, I visualized having a beautiful white smile in my winning moment onstage. When I was excluded or felt awkward in a social setting, I imagined confidently walking into a room and making people feel comfortable and at ease.

Even though *I* believed it was a dream I could achieve, other people didn't. Just like in any sport or subculture, fans, critics, and message boards exist. After I won Miss North Carolina USA, predictions, rankings, and opinions about who would place and win at Miss USA became prevalent. I remember being called "plain, a clapper, average, and big-nosed." I wasn't a front-runner at all. But I didn't let that derail me.

"It's okay," I'd tell myself. "They just don't know yet."

I wasn't on people's radar, but I was on God's radar. You are always on God's radar, too.

Since I won Miss USA, I've been on several judges panels and have seen firsthand that Shandi's words are true. One woman rises to the top by the end of the night. She is the one who sparkles. She has a gleam in her eyes and in her smile. Her aura is aglow. You can't help but be drawn to her. Something about her is captivating and warm. But you can't really put your finger on what it is.

If someone has this type of presence, you may have heard it referred to as having the *it factor*. But I call it the Sparkle Effect and it isn't just for some girls, it's for you, too. The problem is, it's never been defined.

Pageant competitors spend a lot of money for a winning wardrobe, for lessons on hair and makeup, for modeling coaches, and for glamorous headshots. But *the Sparkle Effect is much more than what meets the eye*. It's the radiance, connectedness, and confidence that transcends all other factors. It causes a woman to stand out whether she's onstage, when dating the guy she likes, when going in for an interview, or when vying for a dream.

It's a radiance that must be nurtured from within. The "fake it 'til you make it" strategy will get you only so far toward reaching your goals. A true winner in life has sparkle about her all the time, whether she is performing or serving, whether the lights are on her or she is in a season of hidden preparation. She has the Sparkle Effect on everything she does. But what is it? How does one get it?

When I got to the Miss USA competition, I didn't have the most expensive gown, the biggest cheering section, the most fans, or even the money to buy everything I needed. What I relied upon was my dream, my faith, my persistence, my resilience, and my God of promises.

I have spent the last years contemplating what defines the mysterious Sparkle Effect. I'm convinced that it starts with your relationship with God and the truth found in His Word for you. I will explain as we go along, because it can work for you. You will be able to believe in your dreams with such fervor that nothing or no one can shake them. You will truly know and be confident in who you are created to be. No matter what your dream is, having the Sparkle Effect is the secret to living it out.

You don't have to fake it anymore. You don't have to rely on the wrong things to give you confidence. You don't have to feel the pressure of "turning it on," because when you step into your royal identity, the Sparkle Effect will naturally flow from within. This journey is going to demystify what it takes to have the qualities of a woman who stands out with radiance beyond beauty.

> *You don't have to feel the pressure of "turning it on," because when you step into your royal identity, the Sparkle Effect will naturally flow from within.*

The Sparkle Effect is powerful and attainable. All you need is an open mind, a right heart, and a willing spirit. The little girl inside you, full of wonder and hope, is waiting. The world needs you.

Are you ready to discover your true identity?

The thirty-one chapters of this book will each highlight a quality of one who sparkles; amplify that quality with prayer; and supercharge its effect with Wonder Words. You'll confidently grow in the embodiment of each quality and have the Sparkle Effect by seeking God through the Word and prayer. This journey isn't about becoming someone you aren't. It's about becoming the woman God created you to be.

Releasing your radiance isn't just for your benefit. It's for those you are called to impact as well. God has called you to shine like a city on a hilltop that should not be hidden (Matthew 5:14). It's time to break out of the dullness. It's time to start sparkling.

THE SPARKLE EFFECT

chapter 1

Sparkle with Decisiveness

Believe every day, everything is possible
A magical journey awaits

—*Shannon Saunders, The Glow*

Before we get started, you must decide where you are headed and what your dream is. In order to be successful in anything, we have to zero in on what God wants to accomplish through us. Otherwise, we will be like a feather in the wind, blowing to the left and right in indecisiveness. What dream has He planted in your heart? If you feel unsure in that area, what do you know for sure?

As the prophet Habakkuk wrote in the Old Testament:

Write the vision; make it plain on tablets,
so he may run who reads it.
For still the vision awaits its appointed time;
it hastens to the end—it will not lie.
If it seems slow, wait for it;
it will surely come; it will not delay. (Habakkuk 2:2–3 ESV)

God gives us a vision for our future. I believe God's dream for our lives is often revealed to us as children. When I was a little girl, I had many dreams. I wanted to be a dancer, a Broadway star, an author, a singer, an actress, a lawyer, a politician, and of course, Miss USA. I also secretly wanted to be a princess whisked away to an enchanted kingdom to live happily ever after with a prince. *Do you remember what your dreams were?*

These aspirations have varied based on what season of life I've been in, but there were two constants: to be Miss USA and to marry a prince. I remember doodling my name, "Kristen Dalton, Miss USA," in my notebooks from the time I was twelve years old. I remember my mother reading bedtime fairy tales and Bible stories to us and watching Disney princess movies with my sisters. I was fascinated with the notion of being a princess, which I think is something the little girl in each of us can relate to if we are really honest with ourselves.

One of my absolute favorite things to do as a child was to go through the beautiful, glittering costumes in my mother's big oak chest she turned into a dress-up box. I loved twirling around in her flowing white dress in the living room, wearing it as I ran in the big field behind our backyard and tiptoed my way into the outskirts of the forest. I imagined stories in my head about being in another time period in another land. In every story I made up, I was an advocate for justice, a difference maker, a believer in miracles and true love. The wonderful thing is, I now know those weren't just fairy tales and stories. I can embody the qualities of the heroines I imagined myself to be, and so can you. I encourage you to sit down and remember the dreams of the little girl in you and keep them alive, no matter how difficult or how the world may scoff at them. You were given those visions for a reason.

As life would have it, we grow up and encounter distractions that lead us away from our dreams and goals. As young adults, we suddenly experience how the opinions of others impact us. Failure is painful. We consciously or subconsciously shift our aspirations to fill our need for the approval of others, or in order to prevent the blow of failing at the thing that matters most to us. It's important that we fight against the urge to quit on our true dreams or to stop believing in ourselves, or most importantly, God. You'll find it can be a difficult journey. I have experienced it.

When I was twelve years old, I remember noticing that I wasn't taken seriously by my teachers and the classroom parents because I had blond hair. I dealt with the stereotype that since I was blond and cheerful, I must be dumb. All I wanted was to be smart and taken seriously. I felt inadequate when I didn't pass the test to get into pre-algebra classes with my peers. I began fighting against the labels of others, and what was even more detrimental, my own self-doubts.

Since I didn't qualify to take algebra in middle school, I took it later in high school. I remember coming home to do my homework. Frustration consumed me because I couldn't understand the concepts. I would cry and say things to myself like, "You are so stupid; your brain is so dumb; you'll never prove to everyone that you're smart because you're not!" At one point, I actually set a career aspiration to be a neonatologist, just so I would sound smart. I had no interest in becoming a neonatologist at all, other than because it involved babies. Have you ever done something like this? Have you ever tried to prove something about yourself because you felt inferior or deficient?

In some ways, my desire to prove my intelligence paid off because it kept me motivated and contributed to a résumé of accomplishments. But it would have saved me a lot of tears, heartache, self-loathing, and depression if I had just loved and accepted the imaginative, creative, musical girl God made me to be. I wish I had known sooner that true confidence comes in seeking His approval only. I want to help you understand how God loves the way He made you. Yes, even your perceived weaknesses like algebra.

Ask yourself these questions: What is the deep burning desire in your heart that you wish you could do something about? What innate gifts and talents do you have that the world needs?

Even your birth order can play a role into the dream you are meant to fulfill! As the oldest of four children, I have a big sister's heart for my siblings that has transcended to all women. My heart can't get enough of talking to girls about their value. I experience an adrenaline rush when, through heartfelt conversation, personal coaching, or speaking onstage, I get to help young women become unapologetically confident in who they are.

If you have a passion burning deep within you that has never gone away no matter what the seasons or circumstances you've experienced, you already know what your dream is and the purpose God has stitched into your heart. If you feel unclear about what your calling is, there are powerful ways for you to discern it.

Before moving on in the book, let's get clear on your dream. Create a relaxing space where you can reflect and pray. Grab a journal and pen. Close your eyes each time you ask yourself one of the following questions. Then wait to see what comes to mind:

1. What do you love to do? What do you despise doing?

2. What energizes and excites you? What drains you?

3. What feels easy and natural for you?

4. What do you often find yourself doing or talking about that you can't help?

5. What group of the population do you want to help?

6. Where do you want to see change? How do you want to take part in shaping that change?

7. What do you want to experience and learn?

8. What makes your soul come alive?

I have decided my dream is:

(Note: Don't be frustrated if you are still unclear. If that is the case, it doesn't have to be a specific vocation. Just write what you know to be true. Your dream may be one that reveals itself to you season by season, step by step.)

God has given you access to wisdom and His voice, which will lead you to make strong decisions. Although the Kingdom dwells within you, there are several voices that can drown out the voice of Truth. Voices of parents, teachers, peers, siblings, the enemy, and even your own. While God has placed certain people in your life to guide you, one of the most important skills to develop is the ability to discern God's voice from everyone else's voice, including your own inner thoughts.

> *God has given you access to wisdom and His voice, which will lead you to make strong decisions.*

Hearing many different opinions and judgments can cause confusion. But 1 Corinthians 14:33 says God is not the author of confusion, but of clarity and peace. When you feel confused or lost, that is not from God. The enemy loves to distract us from our true purpose and destiny because it keeps us right where we are—stuck, complacent, and not moving forward. The last thing He wants is for you to use your God-given gifts and talents for Kingdom influence.

Learning how to hear, know, and feel God's voice more and

more has been one of the most wondrous, rewarding journeys that I have experienced. It has proven to make my life more prosperous, protected, and awe-inspiring. I feel like every day is a treasure hunt, and He shows up in sweet, powerful ways when I seek Him.

As His daughter, you have the ability to hear and recognize His voice, too.

I challenge you to get clear on the dream God is calling you to step into. Get into the Word and pray. It is His pleasure to reveal it to you. Make an agreement to partner with Heaven in fulfilling this vision. Then write it down on paper, on a chalkboard, or in your journal. Doodle it every day.

Deciding Your Dream = The Sparkle Effect

Prayer

Dear Father:

Thank You so much for being the ultimate dreamer and dreaming me into life. Thank You, God, for having a precise purpose for my life, and I trust that You will guide me. Lord, please forgive me for doubting You and doubting myself. There have been seasons where I have felt so overlooked and have been distracted by people, circumstances, and self-hate. I am sorry for being so afraid of failure that I have settled for mediocrity in order to stay comfortable. God, I believe that You didn't place a dream in my heart for me to talk myself out of. Even though there have been detours, I have faith that You will always use my mistakes for Your greater glory.

God, thank You for giving me the mind of Christ. Thank You for providing clarity and vision when I ask. Since I am Your daughter, I trust that You speak to me through visions, dreams, Scripture, and strong, convicting feelings. I invite You to open my mind and heart to be receptive to the clarity of Your Word. In Jesus' name, Amen.

Wonder Words

In their hearts humans plan their course, but the Lord establishes their steps.

—Proverbs 16:9

Take delight in the Lord, and he will give you the desires of your heart.

—Psalm 37:4

For, "Who can know the Lord's thoughts? Who knows enough to teach him?" But we understand these things, for we have the mind of Christ.

—1 Corinthians 2:16

chapter 2

Sparkle with Vitality

Remember, you're the one
Who can fill the world with sunshine.

—Snow White

As children, our parents warn us that we aren't invincible. I don't know about you, but I was told to protect my skin from the sun, to eat nutritiously, and not to pick at my zits because it would leave scars. I didn't listen. Why is it when we're teenagers that we think we know more than our parents?

My mom warned me this day would come. The day I regretted not listening to her. I'm sure you've heard similar sentiments before, too. Now that I am grown up, I am actually concerned more about my health, not just what I look like. In my teens and early twenties, my appearance mattered way more to me than my health, and sometimes I went to drastic measures to maintain a certain number on the scale.

I was a cheerleader, on the swim team, and a performer in musical theater—all activities that required physical fitness. I was extremely body conscious. As a matter of fact, food controlled me. I wasn't sure how anyone could eat freely without thinking about how long it would take to work the calories off or about how many grams of carbs they'd just consumed.

During my junior year of high school, my parents got me a gym membership for Christmas. I was excited. I loved the gym so much, I wanted to work there, too. The girls working at the front desk were so fit and pretty. I'd be on the elliptical reading a magazine and watch them get off their shift, drink a protein shake, change into cute workout clothes, and begin their workout.

I wanted to be like them. So after a few months of persistently convincing the manager I was mature enough to be the only high schooler who worked there, he gave me a job. I felt so cool donning my black Gold's Gym tee, khaki shorts, and tennis shoes.

As an employee, I got to try samples of supplements and protein bars. One day on my shift, my manager asked me to try a sample of Thermonex, a fat burner. He couldn't have asked a more eager seventeen-year-old girl. He told me it was safe, so I took it.

Minutes later, I literally felt like I was bouncing off the walls. I was so hyper. For a girl who never drank coffee or sodas, this pill was like taking speed. I loved the way it felt, and in that moment, my use and abuse of fat burners began.

Until then, I was a pretty healthy teenager. But when introduced to the world of diet pills, a lot changed. It started with a whole bottle of Thermonex. I would hide it in my dresser drawer so my family didn't know. I drank protein shakes and ate diet bars instead of eating fruits and vegetables.

I continued in this destructive behavior for a few years. And when I'd get tired of counting calories and measuring my thighs, I would make a bowl of ice cream mixed with peanut butter, Oreos, and chocolate chips. Mmm...it was so yummy—but then I felt guilty. So I'd go on a two-hour run to punish myself.

The crazy part is, I was doing all this insane stuff to my body and I wasn't getting skinny. I actually gained twenty pounds.

I remember coming home from college and noticing my family look at me funny. I had been lying to myself about my clothes not fitting. I thought something was wrong with the dryer in the dorm that was shrinking my clothes. But when I got home, I couldn't hide from myself anymore. Being with family is like looking in a mirror.

I used a variety of fat burners for years. When it wasn't enough anymore, I combined Red Bulls, espressos, and coffees with them, too. Then I'd do at least an hour and a half of cardio. I literally have no idea how my heart didn't explode.

I spent years wreaking havoc and destruction on my body; by speeding up my heart rate with diet pills, consuming fake foods and processed meal replacements, and then forbidding my system to digest food normally by taking laxatives. All because I wanted control in the name of "excellence." Basically, I didn't trust God's design enough.

Realistically, I should have had a heart attack. I could be dead. My body shouldn't be functioning normally after all the trauma I put it through. By the grace of God I'm still here.

When I got deeper into my relationship with God, after the painful breakup I mentioned earlier, God really spoke to me. I cried on my living room floor when He told me He had seen everything I had done to myself. I cried when He told me I was the temple He wanted to live in. He told me if I changed my ways and started trusting Him and caring for my body, even if it meant gaining a few pounds, that He would give me a restart.

It's like He reset my body and made my heart good as new. I had an EKG done and it showed I was in perfect condition. That is grace I didn't deserve.

How do you feel about your body? Do you feel beautiful

in your divine feminine design? How have you been treating your temple? Be soft with yourself, God doesn't want you to be ashamed. He is there to hold you in His arms and give you a restart, too.

We live in a high pressure society riddled with media marketing schemes and Photoshopped images. Forget the fact that these images aren't real. They aren't *you*, and that's what matters. The enemy will use your desire to look like someone you are not to take drastic measures that could possibly kill you. God wants you to be healthy so you can vivaciously live out your purpose.

The enemy will offer you temporary "highs" that feel good now. A stimulant like caffeine, a laxative, a number on the scale, a measuring tape—they all offer control. It feels good to be in control. But when you fail, the enemy riddles you with guilt, shame, and self-punishment.

When we are in control, God isn't.

Having the Sparkle Effect has to do with our character. But our character can't sparkle when we are poisoning our body. It is imperative that you honor the body God specifically designed for you to fulfill your specific purpose. We must care for our temple and steward our health well. Our body is a gift. If we can't manage our own body, how can God trust us to manage our destiny?

> *It is imperative that you honor the body God specifically designed for you to fulfill your specific purpose.*

How you take care of your body today will manifest itself tomorrow, and tomorrow always comes.

Ten Ways to Care for Your Vitality

1. Get seven to nine hours of sleep a night.

2. Exercise at least thirty minutes every day.

3. Enjoy a diet primarily comprised of foods God created and you can't go wrong.

4. Take a great multivitamin and any other vitamins you are deficient in.

5. Wear sunscreen and hats to protect your skin.

6. Drink two liters of water per day.

7. Get an annual physical including every test your insurance will cover.

8. Visit an OB-GYN annually, and get a Pap smear.

9. If you don't listen to your parents, listen to me.

10. Live a natural and holistic lifestyle so your body can reset and all your organs can function properly.

I remember one night at church the Lord spoke to me about my body. I have an affinity for a crisp, cold glass of New Zealand sauvignon blanc. I had been enjoying a glass (or two) of this scrumptious wine almost every night, which I thought was probably not the best thing, but also not terrible. It's embarrassing to admit that I knew God didn't like it. I ignored the promptings and thought I'd get away with it for a while. After all, Jesus did turn water into wine...right? Well, God let me get away with it for a while. I believe He prefers us to use the brain He gave us to choose self-discipline over gluttony, but if we don't get with the program, He is sweet enough to intervene.

That night in worship, I was praying for more of His presence and for the Holy Spirit to speak to me. His response was, "Consecrate your body. Get rid of the spirits to make room for the Spirit." I knew this moment was coming, but I wasn't sure what it would look like. I started crying because of His tender nudge. He was simply saying, "If you want more of Me, make room."

What is God saying to you about your body? Get alone and ask Him. Maybe you're scared to hear His response. Maybe you don't even need to ask because it's that obvious. God's grace will cover you and wash away your sins, but sometimes we are left with the consequences. Don't get to the point that I did. Don't obsess over numbers. Life is too short for that nonsense. Just enjoy a lifestyle that will energize your vitality. Your vitality is crucial to radiating your true identity. Let your eyes shine on the road to your dream.

Vitality = The Sparkle Effect

Prayer

Dear Father:

Thank You for creating me absolutely perfectly. Lord, I ask that You will help me love myself the way You love me. It's easy for me to get caught up in fad diets and the obsession with being a certain size. I hear girls talking about their weight and jean size all the time, and it makes me question my own worth. I ask that You would give me wisdom and long-term vision to realize my health and vitality are much more important than compromising now. God, I want to treat my body as the temple You live in. I want to be a welcoming, nurturing host for the Holy Spirit to want to reside in. Please enable me when I am weak.

Please forgive me for the damage I've already done to myself. Please forgive me for doubting Your artistry when I doubt my fem-

inine design. Everything that flows from Your hands is good and perfect. Thank You for making me wonderfully and fearfully. In Jesus' name, Amen.

Wonder Words

So God created man in his own image, in the image of God he created him; male and female he created them.
—Genesis 1:27

Don't you know that you yourselves are God's temple and that God's Spirit dwells in your midst? If anyone destroys God's temple, God will destroy that person; for God's temple is sacred, and you together are that temple.
—1 Corinthians 3:16–17

Therefore, I urge you, brothers and sisters, in view of God's mercy, to offer your bodies as a living sacrifice, holy and pleasing to God—this is your true and proper worship.
—Romans 12:1–2

Beloved, I pray that all may go well with you and that you may be in good health, as it goes well with your soul.
—3 John 1:2

chapter 3

Sparkle with Style

Perhaps the greatest risk any of us will take is
to be seen as we truly are.

—Cinderella

For the longest time, I didn't have a sense of style. I looked
to other people and trends to decide what I should wear. My sister
Kenzie has the best style. She's always dialed into what's cool or
what will look good. I snuck in her room a lot to scope out her
closet many times as a teenager. She's only a year younger than
me, but she's a lot smaller. I'd try to convince myself I wouldn't
stretch her clothes out, but she got so mad when I did. The reason
I didn't have a sense of my own style is because I was disconnected
from my true self. I shoved that whimsical and over-the-top part
of me down in hopes of creating an image that would be accepted
by my peers.

When I was competing for Miss North Carolina USA, I
wanted to wear a fitted, black gown with a plunging neckline
and a low back. It was the kind of gown I'd seen girls win in so
I thought it was the "right" thing to wear. Plus, I could channel some A-list, red carpet vibes. But when I tried on fitted,

black gowns no one liked me in them. I was insistent, "This is what wins!" Then, one weekend I was modeling for Sherri Hill, a renown gown designer. She brought a dress out for me to try on. It was a sweetheart neckline with a black velvet, rhinestone bodice and a flowy, white silk chiffon skirt. Not at all what I had imagined. But when I tried it on and walked out in it, I came alive. As I've mentioned, I love to twirl so I could work that dress and make it magical. Everyone absolutely loved me in it. I was so scared to choose this dress because two-toned dresses generally didn't win. It also wasn't sexy. But it was elegant, classy, and I could work it. I won in it! But even after I won the state title, I still hadn't learned the lesson. Immediately, I proclaimed I was going to wear a white gown at Miss USA because "that's what wins at Miss USA."

A white dress is exactly what I got. I didn't try to explore other options. I went straight to Sherri Hill and we sketched out a beautiful, white gown design together. I abandoned the idea of a fitted and sexy dress at Miss USA because I'm simply not a sultry girl. I decided to rock the flowy gown, but it simply had to be white. When I got to Miss USA, though, a big surprise awaited me. It was the morning of our official headshots for the program book. I was so excited to finally shoot with the fabulous photographer, Fadil Berisha. Sherri Hill sponsored the shoot, so we got to wear one of her beautiful dresses. When it was my turn, I walked in the dressing room to try on gowns. Sherri pulled a turquoise gown and handed it to me. When I put it on and came out, it seemed like the energy shifted in the room. I looked in the mirror and felt the energy shift within me as well. I felt absolutely radiant. It was as if the very essence of me had been encapsulated in a gown. I was wearing the gown; the gown wasn't wearing me. It was a Cinderella moment. Both Sherri and Fadil said to me, "Kristen, you have to wear this gown to compete!" I thought they were joking. Besides, how could I change gowns at this point in time? I couldn't afford it anyhow. I stood in the mirror feeling absolutely aglow, wearing my favorite color, in a surreal Cinderella moment. But the gown was turquoise. No one had ever won Miss USA in a turquoise gown; it was too risky.

I went to bed that night and couldn't sleep. I couldn't shake the turquoise gown. *How would I pay for it? What if my directors don't like it? What if I take the risk and don't win?* I decided to pray about it. The fact I was even considering changing gowns was out of character for me and scary. The next morning I woke up and even though I felt afraid, my mind had changed. I had to choose the turquoise gown! If I really wanted to be a role model and a leader, I had to take a risk. The risk was going against the grain and being seen for who I truly was. I owned my style as a child, and now at twenty-two years old, it was time to reclaim it. God presented me with two choices: be true to the essence of me or choose what I thought would win. And yes, I believe God is within every detail of our lives, even evening gowns. The turquoise gown captured the essence of me and I had to honor that. If they didn't pick me for being me, at least I wouldn't have regret.

After I won Miss USA, the coolest thing happened. Perez Hilton, one of the judges that night, came up to me afterward and said, "I picked you because you reminded me of Cinderella. You are a real life Disney princess!" His impression spoke to my heart because being a princess is the essence I had tried to hide and stuff down for so long. Finally, on the night that mattered most, I made a decision to stop conforming. I made a decision to be true to the young woman God created me to be...a twirling, whimsical princess.

Another cool thing happened after that. Girls started wearing and winning in colorful gowns! Alyssa Campanella wore emerald green with her fiery red hair. Olivia Culpo wore a Grecian fuchsia number, and Olivia Jordan won in a hot pink ball gown. That had never happened! These colors are not traditional winning colors, so to speak. But they emanated the essence of each brave girl who made a bold move. I'm not saying it's all because of me. But I am saying that one step of bravery to be seen for who you truly are even in your style, can inspire others to do the same. Stepping out may defy the norm or the pattern of what wins.

Are you choosing a style that represents your true essence? Something fun to do is to look up the meaning of your favorite color. It probably represents your personality in some way and you should wear more of it!

Now that you know you can dress to represent the aura of who you are, the second part of sparkling with style is to display your dignity. How we dress is an outward expression that makes an important impression. As much as we hear, "Don't judge a book by its cover," the truth is, people do. Choose a style that enhances your sparkle.

How we dress isn't just about making a good impression; it's an expression of our confidence and self-respect.

When I was in middle school, I didn't feel pretty or confident. Getting attention from boys made me feel good, so I paid attention to what they liked. Having a nice butt and boobs were important to them, so I started wearing clothes that emphasized those things. Well, I didn't have boobs at the time, but I started wearing a padded bra and tight shirts. The video for Christina Aguilera's song "Come On Over Baby" made pleather (plastic leather) pants popular, so I wanted a pair in every color. My mama wouldn't buy them for me, so I convinced my grandma to take me shopping. For some reason shiny, tight, leopard pants didn't raise a blip on grandma's radar and she bought them for me.

I definitely couldn't walk out of my parents' house wearing these pants, so I would roll them up in a ball and hide them in my book bag. I'd scurry to the bathroom and change into my pop star outfit and walk out like I was the hottest thing since sliced bread.

In addition to the shiny leopard pants and short polka-dot skirts, I also caked on layers of makeup. I had really bad acne, so I couldn't just cover it up with concealer; I had to go all out with a full face. You know what I'm talking about.

Once I discovered Britney Spears, I was inspired by her makeup in the music video for "Oops!...I Did It Again." To my delight, *Cosmo* magazine revealed the makeup products she used...or at least that's what I believed. I found all the products at CVS when my mom was out of town: my dad naively bought me a foundation stick, cream bronzer, cream blush, and a ton of black eyeliner. Come to think of it, Britney's makeup artist probably didn't use drugstore makeup. Oh well!

I wanted to look really tan so I wore my foundation a few shades darker and wore frosty lipstick from Bath and Body Works. Truly, any evidence of this time in my life was burned or just never documented because my poor mother was so distressed by how I insisted on walking out the door.

By general perception, I dressed "skanky," or "slutty." Although I looked this way, I didn't act it. I knew how to flirt with a boy, but I never went any further than kissing. But the way I dressed and presented myself caused my peers and teachers to draw other conclusions about me.

In full disclosure, I enjoyed hearing the comments boys made about how I looked. It felt good to get attention and admiration.

But this strategy of gaining confidence lasted only a semester because one day everything changed. I was on the blacktop for recess and this boy was teasing me. I'm not sure exactly how it happened, but he looped his sweatshirt between my legs and pulled it up hard. I remember feeling so violated and dirty. It shook something in me.

From that day forward, I stopped wearing heavy makeup and tight, shiny pants. I made a decision that I needed to dress and carry myself in a way that conveyed I was smart. When we appear not to have self-respect, others seem to have a harder time treating us respectfully.

During that semester, I became a target of dislike and contempt among girls for dressing the way I did. Have you ever felt like girls didn't like you because boys did? It's one thing not to dim your sparkle to make someone else comfortable. But it's another thing when it's less about your sparkle and more about getting attention. I wanted to have girlfriends, so my priorities changed. I started going to Young Life meetings and getting more involved in youth group. I wore overalls and a big silver cross necklace. A little extreme, but I was making an outward statement of my inner change. Have you ever done that? It's not wrong; it just goes to show that the way we dress is a way to communicate what we want people to know about us.

The summer before high school, I literally went back-to-school shopping at Ann Taylor Loft. You know, the preppy store for more mature ladies, not necessarily teenagers. I abandoned the desire for boys to notice me, read books like *I Kissed Dating Goodbye*, and went on a True Love Waits retreat. My priority shifted to gaining the respect and approval of my teachers rather than the attention of boys. My mama was totally down to help me shop for coral capris and sweater sets!

When I moved to Los Angeles and began modeling and commercial acting, I needed to earn favor with my agents and clients to stay on top. I was a Christian, but I didn't know about my royal identity at the time, and my standards began to conform to the world's standards of what was acceptable and normal. Although I didn't struggle much with peer pressure, I did desire approval from authority figures. I guess it could be called adult-pleasing.

One day I was booked on a lingerie job I wasn't comfortable with. I felt hesitant and uneasy, but didn't want to risk displeasing my agent by turning it down. The rate was good, and it's very important not to be difficult or a "diva." I e-mailed my agent before the shoot to get a written confirmation that I would be covered appropriately. She assured me I would be and that this was a great client. So I took the job.

The moment I arrived on set, I saw the wardrobe rack and immediately felt a sinking feeling in my stomach. I remember nervously whispering with the other model about how we both felt uncomfortable, but we still felt the pressure to continue with the shoot. We couldn't turn around and be responsible for burning a client-agent relationship. While shooting, the team was saying, "Gorgeous! Amazing! Wow!" There were several outfits they wanted me to wear that compromised the coverage my agent and I had agreed upon.

I managed to muster up the boldness to insist that I be covered, and they begrudgingly obliged my requests and altered some of the pieces to make this happen. The set, makeup artists, stylists, and photographer were all professional, so my anxiety slowly came down throughout the day. I told myself, "Just get through today and you will be fine. At least it is styled tastefully." I became more comfortable throughout the day, but this was to my detriment later.

The more we do something that doesn't feel right, the more immune to it we become.

Unfortunately, I wouldn't be fine when the shoot was over because photos last forever. What I justified as "styled tastefully" was a far cry from "dressed in dignity." From one shoot in one day, I would have to live with the photos forever. Anytime you shoot with anyone else, whether it be a brand or a photographer, you do not own the images and surrender your rights to them. This is something I was ignorant about at the time. I hope you remember it should you ever do a photoshoot.

This is an example of how we cannot answer to both God and people (Romans 8:8). How can we be a light when we are conforming to the world's standards?

Because of my hurtful experiences with judgmental Christians, I had adopted a more liberal perspective on the topic of modesty. But then I noticed the deeper I fell in love with God, the more I felt a stirring to dress differently. My relationship with God continues to reveal my true identity, which informs my sense of style.

Dressing in dignity isn't about following a rule. It's about being anchored in your regal identity. Just draw closer to God. The closer you are with Him, the more He will reveal to you the essence of who He made you to be.

I learned my first lesson in owning my unique essence at Miss USA.

I don't dress for the approval of anyone now, guys or girls, modest or sexy. I dress to represent who I am and whose I am.

When you are getting dressed, ask yourself, "What does this outfit say about me?" Proverbs 31:25 says, "She is clothed with strength and dignity" (NLT). You are privileged to dress in such a way that conveys the strength and dignified worth of the King's daughter.

> *You are privileged to dress in such a way that conveys the strength and dignified worth of the King's daughter.*

Don't worry about the boys and girls, men and women who may disapprove of you because you aren't dressing in a way that makes them comfortable or happy. When you delight yourself in the Lord, He will make His face shine upon you.

Own your style and what makes you feel lovely. We all have a unique essence. I tend to feel like I am a whimsical princess trapped in a Millennial life, so I wear a lot of long, flowy dresses. What about you? One of my favorite things is helping girls discover who they are in the spirit. If you are feeling stuck on truly knowing who you are, e-mail me and we'll work together through personal coaching! Kristen@SheIsMore.com.

Many times, women who are violated, shunned, or have had terrible things spoken over them tend to lose their self-worth and hide themselves. They lose the beautifully pure sense of who they are or refuse to let the world see it. Hiding feels safer, so they tuck their sparkle under a dowdy appearance, they may put on excess weight, and they don't care about clothing themselves in the best styles for their bodies. Stasi Eldredge writes in more detail about this in her fantastic book *Captivating*.

If this resonates with you, I am sorry for what happened or what was said to you. Your pain is valid and should never be dismissed. I wish I could reach through the pages and comfort you right now and cry along with you. There is restoration available to you. By giving your pain over to your Father, I know you can find your way back to feeling like your true self.

You may know the story of Elizabeth Smart, the fourteen-year-old girl who was abducted from her home and brutally raped, chained, and tortured by her captor for nine hellish months. When she was finally found and restored back to her family, her mother gave her one piece of pivotal advice. She said, "Elizabeth, the best punishment you can give your captors is to live a happy and productive life."

It is time for you to get your revenge on the enemy. You are only imprisoning your heart when you deny yourself happiness. It's time to stop punishing yourself. Jesus already took care of that for you. Will you receive His offer of freedom? Freedom in joy, peace, love, laughter, and happiness?

You deserve to feel great on the inside *and* the outside. You don't have to hide your true self anymore in the way you dress. Everything is interconnected—mind, body, and spirit. It doesn't make us more spiritual to neglect ourselves physically.

I don't need to give you a guideline of what is considered dignified or modest. When you allow Jesus to have your full heart, He will lead you like the gentleman He is. You'll know it's love because it won't feel like a restriction imposed by judgment or condemnation.

What is your essence? What styles make you feel like you are expressing the essence of who God designed you to be? Whatever it is, clothe yourself in strength and dignity and laugh without fear.

Styled in Dignity = The Sparkle Effect

Prayer

Dear Father:

I want to represent You. I want to dress like royalty no matter where I am, no matter what people think. You say that You clothe me in robes of righteousness and I want people to be able to see the beauty and grace of my spiritual clothing just by looking at me.

Will You give me the strength to not conform to the patterns of this world? You call me to be in the world, but not of it. Help me to only want to please you. Give me the courage not to make apologies for the Godly changes I make in my life, even when they make others feel uncomfortable.

Will you give me the boldness to step out and dress in a way that shows who I really am?

Thank You for clothing me and crowning me with tender loving mercies and calling me Your beloved. Amen.

Wonder Words

She is clothed in strength and dignity.

—Proverbs 31:25

Charm is deceitful, and beauty is vain, but a woman who fears the Lord is to be praised.

—Proverbs 31:30

I delight greatly in the Lord; my soul rejoices in my God. For he has clothed me with garments of salvation and arrayed me in a robe of his righteousness, as a bridegroom adorns his head like a priest, and as a bride adorns herself with her jewels.

—Isaiah 61:10

Do not be conformed to this world, but be transformed by the renewal of your mind, that by testing you may discern what is the will of God, what is good and acceptable and perfect.

—Romans 12:2

Likewise also that women should adorn themselves in respectable apparel, with modesty and self-control, not with braided hair and gold or pearls or costly attire, but with what is proper for women who profess godliness— with good works.

—1 Timothy 2:9–10

chapter 4

Sparkle with Beauty

The flower that blooms in adversity is the most
rare and beautiful of all.

—*The Emperor, from Mulan*

Not only is it *okay* to take pride in your feminine design
and celebrate your beauty, but it is *important*. You may wonder,
Doesn't that make me vain? Aren't Christian women supposed to be humble and plain?

Inner beauty will never fade away, and noble character is priceless. But that doesn't mean we should take the conversation out
of context and let ourselves go. You may hear some Christians
say women shouldn't care about our appearance by quoting this
verse, "Do not let your adornment be merely outward—arranging the hair, wearing gold, or putting on fine apparel—rather
let it be the hidden person of the heart, with the incorruptible
beauty of a gentle and quiet spirit, which is very precious in the
sight of God" (1 Peter 3:3–4 NKJV).

Let's break it down. Some may conclude that this means we
shouldn't take care of our outward beauty. But Peter doesn't say
that at all. The verse says do not let your beauty *merely or only* be

outward. When we focus only on external beauty, the imbalance opens the door to vanity and insecurity. Peter is saying that unfading beauty is in our heart and spirit. He is reminding us to focus on adorning our inner beauty *along* with our outer beauty. It's always all about balance and motives.

What does that look like? Confidence is holistic. The way God made us is holistic. He created our mind, heart *and* our face, hair, eyes, nose, lips, and every other physical attribute. A woman who sparkles has a quiet confidence and feels secure in her divine, feminine design. She doesn't say things like, "I wish I could get my nose done," or "If only I had a different body type, then I'd look good in skinny jeans." We've all been there and spoken unlovingly over ourselves, myself included.

> *A woman who sparkles has a quiet confidence and feels secure in her divine, feminine design.*

I'm sorry, but nothing is more unbecoming than a woman who whines about her looks. I know, I know, you have been led to believe this makes you appear humble and self-deprecating but that is a lie. It's really a technique women employ to make sure all her friends don't feel intimidated by her or accuse her of overconfidence.

When someone compliments you, graciously say, "Thank you." God absolutely loves beauty. Look at the world around you. He made the flowers and butterfly wings, and He paints gorgeous sunsets and sunrises. When He created Eve, she was the crown of creation. Satan hated her because she competed with his beauty. Why in the world would God want you to downplay your beauty? You are allowed to believe you are beautiful and to take care of yourself. Don't let lies from the enemy tell you otherwise.

Here are a few reasons we hide our beauty:

- We believe that if we don't have a stereotypical kind of beauty like a model, actor, dancer, cheerleader, or beauty queen, then we don't have permission to be beautiful. We think beauty is for some people, but not us.
- As I said in the last chapter, women who have been violated or abused tend to either engage in an abusive cycle or hide themselves entirely.
- Some women believe it is offensive or bad to be beautiful.
- If being beautiful has made you a target of jealousy or bullying among other women, dulling yourself down might seem like a good escape, but I have personally learned that doing that isn't serving anyone, especially yourself.
- Women who make it their mission to be taken seriously and accomplish a lot can tend to overload their schedule with commitments and are so busy fulfilling them, they neglect themselves in order to get everything done.

It is not wrong or sinful to be beautiful. It is a gift and God loves beauty.

Song of Solomon 4:7 says, "You are altogether beautiful, my darling; there is no flaw in you" (NIV). You are worthy of being and feeling beautiful. Maybe you were never told you were beautiful and you don't feel like beauty is for you. Maybe you think it's only for certain people. But whether you have ever been told you are beautiful or not, God says you are lovely, captivating, and flawless. He looks at you adoringly. Everything you do and the relationships you develop should align with what God says about you.

The way we present ourselves expresses much about what we believe. Some women mask their natural beauty with layers of makeup. I have been guilty of it. Some women don't wear a drop of makeup. Both women may be trying to hide their true beauty. Don't get me wrong; we should all feel confident enough to walk out of the house without makeup. Most days, I don't wear it if I don't have to. The point is, whether or not we are wearing makeup, if we're doing it because of insecurity or a wrong belief, then our eyes are most likely not sparkling. I have been in both places before. What about you?

A woman with the Sparkle Effect is just as aware of her physical traits as she is of her inner gifts. She knows how to accentuate them to honor her divine design.

For most of my life, I have been self-conscious of my nose, skin, and thighs. My sisters have perfect, small noses and flawless skin. I have a wide nose and have struggled a lot with acne, even as an adult. For so long, I complained about my nose and imagined what it would look like with a little plastic surgery. To my relief, I learned about contouring when I was given a contour pallet with an instruction page on how to "skinnify" your nose. Every time I had a modeling job, I asked the makeup artist to contour my nose—but sometimes they accidentally made it look bigger!

I used to hate my hips and thighs and didn't wear skinny jeans when they became popular because they made my hips look bigger. I've always worn flares because they balance out the size of my thighs—at least that's what I thought. When I tried to lose weight, I would measure my thighs to see if they were getting smaller. I envied girls who had skinny legs and wished I could trade with them.

It's really sad; I spent so much time focusing on disliking and changing my nose and thighs, instead of praising God for making me wonderfully and fearfully. I was bullying myself rather than speaking life to myself. I was basically partnering with the enemy to condemn the way God designed me. Who was I to decide my facial features and body parts weren't cute and lovely?

I wondered how things might change if I started thinking differently about my nose and thighs. I decided to start agreeing with what God said about me and speaking it out loud. When I did my makeup or washed my face, I'd say, "I love my nose, I have such a cute, button nose. It makes me look younger." When I got dressed, I'd say, "Thank You, God, for making my thighs strong and able. Thank you for giving me two legs that I can depend on to get me where I need to go. I love my thighs; they are perfectly shaped for what I need to do."

It was amazing how drastically this made a difference. Rather than punishing the physical parts of ourselves we don't like, why don't we love them and be kind with them instead? I felt happier, more confident, and altogether less hung up on myself. When we own and love how God designed us, we can focus more on what God wants to do through us.

What are your physical hang-ups?

How are you going to start thinking and talking about them to honor God's design of you?

What are your favorite features about yourself?

Here are some ways to celebrate your divine design:

- Acknowledge your eye color. Eyes are very expressive and the windows to our soul. They can be really fun to accentuate with makeup colors to make them pop.

- Lip gloss is a great staple because it's effortlessly pretty and can be used whether you have a full face of makeup on or are just going for the natural look. It's easy to apply and touch up on the go. I love and wear NYX butter glosses. They are inexpensive—you can get them at the drugstore—but they are gorgeous!

- Blush for rosy cheeks is everything. It makes you come alive and look bright, youthful, and glowy.
- You can't go wrong with a great concealer. I would go as far as to say it's necessary. I use Maybelline's Age Rewind concealer under my eyes almost daily unless I'm working out or just running errands. You can also use it on any other spots or lesions that bother you. It awakens your face and helps with dark circles or tired-looking eyes.
- Maintain a healthy-looking haircut that frames your face shape. You want to look fresh and clean all the time, and when you don't have the time, dry shampoo is everything. Batiste is my go-to and can also be found at drugstores!
- If you are blessed with curly hair or freckles, those are things that make you stand out ... rock them!
- Wash your face every morning and thoroughly before bed. Wearing makeup to bed is terrible for your skin and lends to pre-aging. Always wear a daily sunscreen.
- If you struggle with acne, like me, make an appointment with a dermatologist. Just make sure your insurance covers your visit before you go. Acne is no laughing matter. It is medically referred to as acne vulgaris because it is characterized as a skin disease. If you don't take care of it now, it could leave permanent scars and discoloration. You are worth enjoying your skin!

The point of embracing your beauty is to recognize, appreciate, and nurture the special beauty marks God gave you.

Your God-given beauty is powerful and can be used for the good of the Kingdom. Esther was a very beautiful woman, and her beauty gained her a foot in the door with the king of Persia. Her Sparkle Effect radiated through her outer beauty, and the king chose her to be his queen. Her beauty opened the door to a position she used to save an entire race of people. When Abraham's servant set out to find a wife for Isaac, it was Rebecca's beauty that caught his eye and caused him to notice her kindness. He chose her to be Isaac's wife and she then became the mother of Israel. How does God want to use your beauty?

Don't try to be someone you're not. Take time to notice how God designed you and explore how you can celebrate those sweet touches. When you decide to appreciate and rock your unique beauty, God can use it in unexpected ways.

Embracing Your Beauty = The Sparkle Effect

Prayer

Dear Father:

Thank You for making me unique. I am sorry for hiding myself because of painful things that happened to me or ways I have been treated. Today is a new day and I can't move forward without forgiving those who made me feel like it was wrong or offensive to be beautiful. Lord, will You please help me to forgive the people Satan used to corrupt me and make me feel my beauty was perverse?

Also, please forgive me for idolizing beauty. Today, I am taking beauty off the throne and worshipping You, the Beauty Maker, instead. I pray that You will strengthen me to keep my outward adornments in balance with my inner beauty. I know that a gentle and quiet spirit is precious in Your sight.

As You are working on my character, to make it have more and more of the radiance of Christ, I pray that I will better learn to see my beauty through Your eyes. I want to be the best version of myself and for people to see You when they see me. Amen.

Wonder Words

I praise you, for I am fearfully and wonderfully made. Wonderful are your works; my soul knows it very well.

—Psalm 139:14

And the king will desire your beauty. Since he is your lord, bow to him.

—Psalm 45:11

Charm is deceitful, and beauty is vain, but a woman who fears the Lord is to be praised.

—Proverbs 31:30

Behold, you are beautiful, my love, behold, you are beautiful! Your eyes are doves behind your veil. Your hair is like a flock of goats leaping down the slopes of Gilead. Your teeth are like a flock of shorn ewes that have come up from the washing, all of which bear twins, and not one among them has lost its young. Your lips are like a scarlet thread, and your mouth is lovely. Your cheeks are like halves of a pomegranate behind your veil.

—Song of Solomon 4:1–3

And your renown went forth among the nations because of your beauty, for it was perfect through the splendor that I had bestowed on you, declares the Lord God.

—Ezekiel 16:14

chapter 5

Sparkle with Resilience

No matter how your heart is grieving
If you keep on believing
The dream that you wish shall come true

—*Cinderella*

A woman doesn't radiate from the inside out without overcoming adversity or pain. Regardless of where you were born or the socioeconomic status you grew up in, we all experience the fear of rejection and failure. The question is, do we allow ourselves to *experience* the pain of failure? And do we allow ourselves to reach for something our heart desires even when we feel unqualified or unworthy? Take a moment to search your heart with these questions.

Most of us remain in the comfort of what we know works. The risk of failing is too scary. We are afraid to fail because we think it says something bad or affirms something bad about who we are. Don't fall into that common trap. You aren't common. Does failing outweigh the risk of not living out your calling?

The looming threat over my life from ages twelve through twenty-one was the word *rejection*. I had this dream of being Miss USA, and I researched everything about the women who held the Miss USA title. I studied their bios, résumés, accomplishments, and quotes from interviews. I made lists of short-term and long-term goals to accomplish so that by the time I was ready to compete, I had hopefully developed the character and experience it took to succeed. Having a list of goals from a young age was a good thing, but it also meant that I heard the word *no* a lot.

I grew resilient through rejection believing I was a winner in the making. You can believe this way, too.

I competed in nine pageants before making it to the big stage. Every time I competed, I prepared and tweaked my résumé, talent, styling, and interview skills better than before. I remember standing onstage waiting to hear the results, hoping the judges had chosen me. Each time, I was a runner-up. I was escorted away to witness the winner in her well-deserved moment of victory. The thoughts that floated in my mind were, *What am I missing? What do they not see? Am I not smart enough or well spoken enough? Why don't the judges like me? Am I just meant to be a runner-up?*

What I learned through these experiences is the value in not always winning. Losing is an opportunity to grow in character and skill. If I had won on my first attempt or given up when I didn't win the Strawberry Festival Princess pageant, I wouldn't have taken the hard, honest look at myself and received the mental toughness I needed at Miss USA. You, too, can build resilience and embolden the path to your future by not letting setbacks stop you from pursuing your ultimate dream. The perspective you gain from losing is a gift to make you more prepared for the big leagues. Losing is not failure. It's training ground.

Many of us have the dream and feel the magic of our destiny swirling in the core of our being. It's so alive in us that it's the one thing that gives us the hope to keep going. When something is that active inside us, it may seem it should manifest in our lives quickly. It feels like we are ready to be promoted to that level of greatness. So why does it seem we keep failing time after time?

God will use that fire inside you to motivate you to put yourself out there. It's almost as if we need to believe the dream is at our fingertips in order to get us to take the risks and leaps of faith. But God works in mysterious ways, and until the timing is divine, He fiercely protects His daughters from unforeseen harms.

Even in the moments that feel like rejection, it's usually God's protection. He wouldn't allow me to be elevated to the level of competing at Miss USA until I had the resiliency and maturity to match the task. That could only come through the character and skill refinement that resulted from failing over and over again.

I recently created my own online magazine for women called SheIsMore.com. In developing content for the magazine, I have come to realize that failure doesn't exist when you have the right perspective. I write articles from my heart and then surrender the results to God. If a topic I really love doesn't get a lot of views, I've learned not to question whether or not I am supposed to write. I use each article and video I create as practice to get better and as a chance to understand what matters to my readers. No matter the results, my efforts always provide an opportunity for growth.

On the flip side, no matter how hard we try, sometimes our dreams don't come to pass and it can be very devastating. This happened to my younger sister, Julia. Her dream was also to be Miss USA. She actually was second runner-up to Miss Teen USA before I competed at Miss North Carolina USA, so she was successful in the pageant world before I was. It was a dream we shared and bonded over as young girls.

We would practice our swimsuit walk together in the family bonus room to our favorite Top 40 songs. We used a broken-off leg from our mini trampoline as the microphone to ask each other the "final question" and practice our onstage answers. She was a pro, much better than me. She is calm, level-headed, extremely intelligent, and confident. So when she decided she was ready to start on the path leading to Miss USA, I just knew she was destined to win. It would be such a sweet story, too, right? Two sisters sharing the same title.

We literally ate, slept, and breathed her dream. I felt like I was competing all over again because I wanted it just as badly for her as she did.

I took a week off to be in the pageant's host city, Baton Rouge, in the days leading up to the telecast. We were so excited the moment was finally here! But things started spiraling out of Julia's favor from the first day. The important thing to know is sometimes things happen that are out of our control. I felt so sick to my stomach the whole week leading up to the pageant that I lost seven pounds.

She didn't make the top 15. As a matter of fact, it seemed she was behind all the girls all night. Even from the second row, I couldn't see her.

If you are in pageants, you probably understand the gravity of the situation. If you aren't and you think I sound like a crazy pageant mom...well, that is probably a little true. But to shed some light on how Julia felt, imagine your dream. Every time you work out, you see that dream in your mind and it motivates you to run a little faster. Every time you hear a "NO," you remember your dream and it gives you hope. Every time you face a temptation, you rethink it and say "NO" because it wouldn't be worth risking your dream.

You don't just prepare for a year. You prepare for years and years. Come on, you know what I'm talking about. Regardless if you have a clear dream, you still do things and make certain decisions with some hope in mind.

For Julia, her dream of becoming Miss USA was the hope that kept her going through betrayal, an abusive relationship, and a long period of illness. What's worse is that she felt to the very core of her being that it was God who told her to dream for it.

When all the work, visualizing, preparing, and hoping for your childhood dream is negatively affected, it can be painful. You feel helpless and confused and wonder if you did something wrong or heard God wrong.

Sometimes we don't actually realize that dream because God had a different purpose for that journey. We may never understand it as hard as we try. Julia felt teased and humiliated. Have you ever felt this way? Have you ever felt completely hidden?

Take heart, baby girl. In your disappointment, it's tempting to run *from* God, but that's when it's crucial to draw near *to* God. Don't worry, you can tell Him how you feel, anger, confusion, and all. He cries when we cry. He is our comforter; He says He will hide us in the shadow of His wings. It's in the moments of heartache and pain that we have a life-defining choice to make. Will we allow it to harden and jade our hearts? Or will we choose to let it refine our hearts with resilience?

Resilience is like a swan. Water turns to glistening beads when splashed upon her wings. She's strong, yet still elegant in the way she swims along. She doesn't harden, quit, or show out in the face of adversity.

Sometimes heartbreaking, unpredictable things will happen on the road to our dream. We can't control everything, but we can decide how we will respond. In Julia's case, she pressed back into God after a period of grieving and processing. Now, He has redirected her and given her special favor and accelerated promotion in a career that fulfills other dreams to travel all over the country and do meaningful work.

Regardless of how dramatic or small your experience has been with rejection, the way you handle it is what matters. You can't fail if you perceive every *try* as an opportunity to bounce back on the path that leads you to becoming the best version of yourself.

> *You can't fail if you perceive every try as an opportunity to bounce back on the path that leads you to becoming the best version of yourself.*

Commit to changing your view of rejection and failure. It's only the end of the world and your dream if you let it be. Use redirection and rejection to your advantage and start taking leaps of faith. God can do great things with a resilient attitude.

Resilience = The Sparkle Effect

Prayer

Dear Father:

Thank You so much for creating me for such an amazing purpose that will change people's lives. God, thank You for Your perfect timing and I trust that it's always in my best interest. Thank You for protecting me in the heavenly realms when I am rejected by people on earth.

God, I ask that You help me walk in the truth that in Christ, I have the power to renew my perspective on failure. Help me to re-

alize that every time I feel overlooked for another opportunity, You see me clearly. You are holding me in the palm of Your hand.

God, thank You for doing amazing things with my obedience. I pray that You will infuse me with the gift of faith, which will lead me to obey Your promptings, and which will diffuse any trace of fear trying to stop me. God, thank You for seeing me when no one else seems to. When traces of doubt creep into me, help them to be overcome by Your delight in me.

Thank You for sustaining me to develop the resilience and wisdom that usher in the fullness of my destiny in Your perfect timing. Amen.

Wonder Words

My flesh and my heart may fail, but God is the strength of my heart and my portion forever.

—Psalm 73:26

For the righteous falls seven times and rises again, but the wicked stumble in times of calamity.

—Proverbs 24:16

Let not your hearts be troubled. Believe in God; believe also in me. In my Father's house are many rooms. If it were not so, would I have told you that I go to prepare a place for you? And if I go and prepare a place for you, I will come again and will take you to myself, that where I am you may be also. And you know the way to where I am going.

—John 14:1

chapter 6

Sparkle with Self-Worth

Sometimes the right path is not the easiest one.

—*Grandmother Willow, from Pocahontas*

In every one of us, there is a desire to stand out. We also want to be accepted. Sometimes, our desire to be accepted outweighs our desire to stand out as our true selves. Being accepted feels safer and less risky. This is the defining moment we may choose to compromise who we are, which ultimately affects our dream. But you don't have to fall into this trap. There is a way to guard yourself against the temptation to blend in. *The key is to set standards for your life.* Setting standards means you know your self-worth. Taking the time to set standards and write them down gives you more power and probability in staying true to yourself and your dream. It gives you a foundation to propel you upward and a blocking point to prevent you from falling below.

I was in the seventh grade when I set my first list of life-defining standards. Usually, we might think a confident or popular girl would have the boldness to set standards for her life. But I wasn't confident or popular.

My family had moved to a new town for my father's job. It was a great promotion for him, we were living near the beach, our house was bigger, and my three siblings and I got our own bedrooms. But when you're in the middle of puberty starting middle school in a new town, all that matters is that you have clear skin, friends, and that boys like you. At least, that suddenly seemed really important to me.

My entire world and my notion of normal had been taken away from me with the move. I would have to completely start over knowing absolutely no one. How in the world was I going to manage the first day? Who would I talk to before the bell rang? My mother dropped me off in front of the school, and as I walked toward the blacktop where all the kids hung out before class, the churning feeling in the pit of my stomach balled into a big knot. Every part of my nervous self was screaming to turn around and run back into the car.

Please bell, ring. Please let it be eight fifteen already; please don't make me stand out here alone in this crowd.

It maybe would have been better if I were proud of my outfit. *Why am I wearing Keds? Oh gosh, why didn't I know I was supposed to wear rainbow flip-flops?*

It might have been better if I'd had long, flowing hair. *Oh, why did I ask my mom to give me a* Something About Mary *haircut? I look like a boy. Please Lord, just let me melt into the ground.*

It might have been better if my face had been clear and pretty. But it had been attacked by a fleet of mosquitoes all summer. Well not really a fleet of mosquitoes, it was acne. But it may as well have been, given the appearance of my irritated skin. *I should smile and act friendly. Oh wait, I can't smile. It hurts. Ugh, I can see the mound on my cheek in my periphery . . . and my skin is cracking. I overdid it with the Retin-A again.*

Before we moved, a boy I had a crush on called me a dog. Suddenly those names he called me started floating around in my head. All I could see in the physical realm affirmed that I was low on the social chain and uninvited.

Who was I to set standards for my life?

Thankfully, my parents made it a priority to find a church home for us in our new town. We visited a new church every Sunday. Meanwhile, I couldn't catch a break from the dreaded experience of walking into a room alone where everyone knew each other, knee deep in very important conversations about teenage matters. I was resigned to sympathy conversations with the teacher or adult in the room.

But finally, we found a church where my sister, Kenzie, and I didn't run in the bathroom and hide every time we got dropped off for youth group. Some girls from school were in this youth group, and they even went to a smaller Bible study just for girls, so I made acquaintances and that improved my school experience. I decided to join the girls' Bible study group. We met every Wednesday night at the youth group leader's house. His wife was the leader. I loved Bible study so much. Talking about God, Jesus, and the Word made me so excited. I felt so peaceful; Wednesday nights were my haven.

One night I said to my leader:

"I wish I could be in Bible study and talk about God all day, every day."

She replied matter-of-factly, "Well, you can't do that. You have to go out into the world and live a normal life."

She made a valid point. But I wonder how my life would have been different if she had encouraged me to go to seminary or to become a Bible teacher. Do you ever wonder things like that? About how things might be different if someone in your life encouraged the budding aspirations within you?

One Wednesday night was different from the others. We had a guest speaker that night. I sat there mesmerized with my journal open and pen feverishly writing as she spoke. I was a girl confused by the tension of a future dream, the untainted fearlessness I had as a child, and my present reality.

I felt like she was speaking directly to me when she said, "You are worthy of setting standards even if it doesn't make sense now. God loves you so much. You are filled with the fullness of God. Because you are full, you never have to compromise for a boy, to fit into the popular crowd, or to be accepted by anyone. His dream for your life is so much more important than that."

It all resonated with me. Even though I couldn't see evidence of my value based on my current, external circumstances, her message rang true in the caverns of my soul.

That message is for you, too. You are worthy of setting standards for your life.

The speaker told us something else that night. She told us that we were worthy of saving our sexual purity for marriage one day. She explained how sex is a beautiful gift created by God to consummate two souls together under covenant.

The whimsical, Disney-loving side of me ignited at the thought of this. The idea of saving this gift for my future husband seemed so romantic and sacred. It also seemed like a good way to find out if a guy truly respected and valued me. So, that night, I made a decision to believe God made me worthy of setting standards that would cultivate space for His blessing. I wrote the promise in a letter:

Dear God:

I promise I will not drink alcohol, try drugs, or smoke, and I will save the gift of sex for my husband.

Love,
Kristen

Then I folded it up and placed it in an envelope and gave it to my Bible study leader. In that season of my life, I didn't feel beautiful, confident, or happy, but I made a decision that I would believe God's Word instead of my feelings. From that point on, the vow was sealed, never to be broken.

God's Word is true and you can cling to what *He says* about you even when *you feel* differently. He says you are more precious, more valuable than rare jewels! That means you can treat yourself that way. It means you are worthy of choosing relationships with people who treat you with honor and value.

There may be naysayers who will try to discourage you from living a compromise-free life. So many people scoffed at my decisions not to drink, try drugs, or have sex. I used their doubt to motivate me even more. You can, too! *Don't let naysayers break you, let them catapult you.*

By God's grace, I was able to stay true to my vow throughout high school and college. Temptations presented themselves, but the hope in my dream and the standards I set helped me remain steadfast. I knew where I was going. To me, nothing was worth compromising the dream in my heart, the kind of woman I wanted to become, or the life I wanted to live. The same goes for you.

The woman God made you to be deserves to set standards, too. The dream and destiny for which you were set apart deserve to be set up for success. Without unnecessary, self-inflicted distractions and detours.

She who lives without standards is a woman in danger. Without standards, it's much easier to submit to our feelings. Our feelings will deceive us, and the enemy will present shiny distractions like a wrong guy or wrong group of friends that we will attempt to fill that desire to be accepted. In times of desperation or emptiness, we'll accept the first thing that invites us in. This is why we need standards to protect us from impulsive decisions when we are feeling weak and vulnerable.

You are never too old or too young to set standards for your life. Even if you feel you have already messed up or your character and reputation have been compromised, you can decide to start fresh this very moment. The Word says God's mercies are new every morning. Every single morning, you get a brand-new chance.

Standards may affect different aspects of life. Whether it is regarding romantic relationships, careers, friendships, family, finances, dealing with a boss, teacher-student dynamics, your extracurricular commitments, or your faith, standards are generally rooted in respect, integrity, and love.

One area in which women often have trouble maintaining their standards is romantic relationships. Have you ever watched yourself fall for someone who was terrible for you? Did you wonder how in the world you got so deeply into it? You're not alone. And the reason this happens is that love is blind and feelings are deceiving. Before we know it, we are justifying someone's behavior and making excuses for them. Even the strongest, securest women have been here, so don't feel any guilt or shame.

The key to avoiding this situation is to set standards for romantic relationships *before* we get into them. Ask yourself: What are my nonnegotiables? What is acceptable? What is unacceptable? Then make a list of your answers.

Even if you have some idea of what you want your future husband to be like, it is important that you define the specific traits your life partner should have. After my year as Miss USA and I had moved to Los Angeles, I joined a small women's Bible study. This was the second Bible study in which I made a list of standards. One week, we were required to make a "husband list" for homework. It couldn't simply be a list of basic traits he should have—for example, "he must be handsome or kind." No, we had to be specific. An example of something we'd list would be, "A man who has a calm temperament and handles stress well." This may sound silly, but you need to put the important qualities you desire into writing so that they hold you accountable. Specific standards also give you heightened discernment in dating situations.

Let's be honest, it can be easy to let something slide or dismiss a red flag when a cute guy tells us yummy, fluttery words we want to hear. But it is an ugly situation when we let our hearts get too attached to someone who ultimately won't take care of it. The list keeps your standards in check and can help you quickly discern whether or not a guy gets a second date. It protects your heart against unnecessary wear and tear. In fact, your heart is so important that God says, "Guard your heart above all else, for it determines the course of your life" (Proverbs 4:23 NLT).

I encourage each of you to make a husband list, too. Three months after I made mine, I met my future husband, and not only did he possess every single character trait on my list of important qualities, he was more. I'm not saying this is a surefire result because each of our stories is different. But I am saying that God "...is able to do immeasurably more than all we ask or imagine, according to his power that is at work within us" (Ephesians 3:20 NIV).

Choosing who you will partner with the rest of your life is one of the biggest decisions you will ever make. Too many of us are settling for less than God's best because we don't know exactly how He desires for His daughters to be treated. Your husband list is going to have unique traits according to who you are, and your quirks, likes, and dislikes. But there are some Godly fundamentals to help you set a framework of nonnegotiables for your future husband. Based on Scripture, here is a list of nonnegotiables you can use as a guideline:

1. He is an active believer.

Do not be yoked together with an unbeliever . . . For what agreement is there between the temple of God and idols?
—2 Corinthians 6:14–16

Issues and conflict are bound to arise in marriage, so it is crucial that there is a common foundation on which to hold your relationship accountable. The last thing you want to be fighting about is your faith, whether or not to pray, and your viewpoints on religion. Believe me, I've been there before. It is exhausting.

2. God is the center of his life.

With wisdom are riches and honor, enduring wealth and prosperity. My fruit is better than fine gold; what I yield surpasses choice silver.
—Proverbs 8:18–19

Your partner seeks God's wisdom in all the decisions he makes.

3. He has integrity and does not put himself in tempting situations.

Keep to a path far from evil, do not go near the door of that house, lest you give your best strength to others.
—Proverbs 5:8–9

Your partner should be a man who guards you against harm and protects the relationship.

4. He seeks Godly mentorship and sound counsel.

The way of fools seems right to them, but the wise listen to advice.

—Proverbs 12:15

It is important that your man is wise in realizing he can't carry the weight of the world on his shoulders. When he is surrounded by men who are older than him who can offer advice, prayer, and mentorship when times are tough, he can be a better husband to you.

5. He is slow to anger.

A hot-tempered person stirs up conflict, but the one who is patient calms a quarrel.

—Proverbs 15:18

There is peace in knowing your man holds an even temperament even when he is provoked. A man who allows his feelings, emotions, and anger to determine his actions typically has tarnished relationships and is not spiritually healthy to be with you or to start a family.

6. He holds strong conviction on the sacredness of fidelity.

May your fountain be blessed and may you rejoice in the wife of your youth . . . May you be ever captivated by her love. Why be captivated, my son, by an adulteress?

—Proverbs 5:18–20

A man is wise when he understands that infidelity and looking for pleasure outside of the marriage only bring strife. God actually calls him to rejoice over you all of his days.

7. He honors your heart and emotional well-being.

Let them be yours alone, never to be shared with strangers.
—Proverbs 5:17

Love each other deeply because love covers all wrongs.
—1 Peter 4:8

I hated when a guy I was dating exposed my embarrassing moments or the private matters of our relationship with his friends. His picking on you may seem cute and funny at first, but it will get old after a while. In life, you should feel honored and safe knowing you can always trust your man to cover and speak well of you. And this will be a characteristic he will exhibit early on.

8. He is disciplined in living a life of integrity.

He will die for lack of discipline, led astray by his own great folly.
—Proverbs 5:23

Watch how a man handles temptation or sticky situations that test his character. Does he choose to do what's right even when no one is watching? It is imperative to observe these things because it will indicate if you can trust his decision making. When you're married, almost all of his decisions impact you.

9. He has a solid work ethic.

A little sleep, a little slumber, a little folding of the hands to rest—and poverty will come upon you like a thief and scarcity like an armed man.

—Proverbs 6:10–11

Your husband should be committed to being a good provider. Look for a guy who works diligently.

10. He pursues and loves you passionately.

Pursues: *So Jacob worked seven years to pay for Rachel. But his love for her was so strong that it seemed to him but a few days.*

—Genesis 29:20

Loves: *Husbands, love your wives, just as Christ loved the church and gave Himself up for her.*

—Ephesians 5:25

The man you marry should make you feel loved like you've never felt before. Safe, accepted, desired, nurtured, protected, and comforted. Jesus loves us deeply; He loves us so fiercely that He willingly gave up His life to save us.

11. He romances you.

Let him kiss me with the kisses of his mouth—for your love is more delightful than wine.

—Song of Solomon 1:2

Place me like a seal over your heart, like a seal on your arm; for love is as strong as death, its jealousy unyielding as the grave. It burns like blazing fire, like a mighty flame.

—Song of Solomon 8:6

I know women who feel guilty or wrong for desiring romance in their relationship, as if they don't deserve it. But God desires for your heart to be romanced, just as He longs to romance us.

12. He is humble and can admit when he is wrong.

Pride comes before destruction, and an arrogant spirit before a fall.

—Proverbs 16:18

There is nothing worse than a petty conflict blowing out of proportion because your partner refuses to admit he is wrong. Taking responsibility for his actions and apologizing for his mistakes are signs of a real man.

No person will be perfect, and extending grace is imperative in a flourishing relationship. That being said, this list is to give you a basic framework of character traits to look for or recognize in determining whether to move forward in a relationship. Of course, use common sense when someone amazing walks into your life but wasn't exactly what you dreamed up. God surprises us, but always gives us what we need.

For I feel a divine jealousy for you, since I betrothed you to one husband.

—2 Corinthians 11:2

Ultimately, your Father wants you to be treated in a way that mirrors Christ's love for you. It is up to you to *believe* you are worthy, to set the standard, and to have the faith that God works in perfect timing to introduce you to your husband.

On its own, that a man is a Christian doesn't mean he is your perfect husband. Just because a man is a Christian does not mean he is Godly or even good for you. Most of my worst dating experiences were with Christian men. I got tired of it. So when I met a nonbeliever who I enjoyed and who was kinder to me than any believer I had dated, I wavered.

And my decision to stray from my standards resulted in a three-year, committed relationship that progressed to marriage discussions and planning a future, and to me compromising my relationship with God. The only way I could make my relationship with him work was to let go of the one with God.

The period of waiting before we find *the one*, distractions, and doubt may cause us to compromise our standards too early. But those who do not give up or grow weary of doing good will reap rewards in the right time.

There are some things we can learn from the mistakes of others and from the Bible to guard our lives. There are other things we have to learn on our own.

When we truly know who we are and trust in God, we won't succumb to the pressure to do something that doesn't feel right. We won't give up too soon or compromise who we are. We have to trust God more than we want our desires.

Maybe you're thinking, *Oh my gosh, life will be no fun. People are right when they say being a Christian is so restrictive.* But the whole point of setting your standards high and abiding by them is so you can avoid living with unnecessary regret, shame, and guilt that often come with living outside of God's boundaries. He gives us the gift of a life map so we can avoid as many traps and landmines as possible. He loves and wants the best for you. Your best life is the one God has planned for you—better than your most wonderful dreams.

I like the way it's put in Ezekiel 20:11–12. It says, "There I gave them my decrees and regulations so they could find life by keeping them. And I gave them my Sabbath days of rest as a sign between them and me. It was to remind them that I am the LORD, who had set them apart to be holy" (NLT). Verse 13 goes on to say, "They wouldn't obey my regulations even though obedience would have given them life" (NLT). You see, just like a parent who protects us from harm and evil, God sets standards for us out of love.

Matthew 7:13 says, "Enter through the narrow gate. For wide is the gate and broad is the road that leads to destruction, and many enter through it" (NIV). Jesus wants us to know that following the masses, the crowd, or even our own justification of sin will only cause destruction, pain, and chaos. That is the opposite of the life He came to give us.

Some may argue, "Well, if I don't try something out and make my own mistakes, how will I ever learn?" I'd say, "You absolutely can learn from your own mistakes. But next-level wisdom is learning from other people's mistakes and trusting God enough to follow His ways." We are going to make plenty of mistakes without making them stubbornly for the sake of "experience." There are some experiences we don't need to have. The Lord will absolutely restore, cleanse, and heal you from any misstep with a sincere and repentant heart, but it's always better to be *proactive* instead of *reactive*. I write to you in hopes that this message will help spare you as many avoidable mistakes as possible on your journey.

In my case, after being in a relationship with a nonbeliever, I had to go through the excruciating heartache of breaking up with him. It was by far the most painful breakup I ever went through. I loved him. In our relationship, I lost parts of my true self and compromised my value, which affected other decisions in my life.

I could have been proactive in trusting God and waiting for the husband He had already chosen for me. Instead I found myself in *reactive* mode working to clean up the mess in my heart and the residual damage it had caused in my life. Have you been there before?

The Bible lays it out in 1 Corinthians 6:9–11:

Don't you realize that those who do wrong will not inherit the Kingdom of God? Don't fool yourselves. Those who indulge in sexual sin, or who worship idols, or commit adultery, or are male prostitutes, or practice homosexuality, or are thieves, or greedy people, or drunkards, or are abusive, or cheat people—none of these will inherit the Kingdom of God. Some of you were once like that. But you were cleansed; you were made holy; you were made right with God by calling on the name of the Lord Jesus Christ and by the Spirit of our God. (NLT)

The Kingdom of God in this Scripture references our ability to access the pure joy, power, radiance, and peace from Heaven during this life. We won't get to tap into the magnificence the Kingdom offers if our lives and hearts are consistently muddled with regret.

We can't serve two gods. We either love the Creator with all our heart and mind. Or we are torn between our love for creations that will never make us whole. Straddling a middle road is dangerous and won't get you anywhere worth going.

You do have a dream worth setting standards for and never

compromising. You have a life full of God's promises and an irrevocable call. The question is, how will you get there? How long
will it take?

Make a decision today that you are worthy of setting standards
for your life. Then, make a vow and write a letter to God.

> *Make a decision today that you are*
> *worthy of setting standards for*
> *your life.*

A few examples of standards you may want to include in your vow
are:

1. I will not drink to the point of drunkenness.

2. I will not use drugs.

3. I will not go to places or parties that cause me or others to
stumble.

4. I will not tolerate mental, verbal, or physical abuse; harass-
ment; or manipulation from anyone.

5. I will honor my body and save sexual purity for marriage.

6. I will only date guys who honor my boundaries and worth.

7. I will surround myself primarily with those who uplift me,
unless for time frames when I am ministering or encouraging
someone.

8. I will make God the center of every aspect of my life.

9. I will be wise in how I use my platform and influence
through social media.

In high school, a friend's mother was driving me home. She
asked me, "Well, what are you going to do when all your friends
are doing it and they pressure you?" I replied, "That's why I have

made a decision before I get into a situation. Then I can be strong and grounded when someone tries to pressure me into sex."

That is exactly why making a resolve in your heart and mind about who you are, what you will and will not do, is crucial to dealing with the pressures of being accepted. You got this, girl. You deserve to stand out as your true self and live a life worthy of your dreams.

Setting Standards = The Sparkle Effect

Prayer

Dear Father:

I lift up my heart to You. I am so beautifully and wonderfully made and designed to live a life that allows light to beam out of me. God, thank You for being the fastest, most gracious forgiver and coverer of my sins. I ask that You would make me feel pure, clean, and gorgeous right now. Alleviate any shame or self-pity from me right now, in Jesus' name. God, strengthen me to evaluate my life with a clear perspective and to see where I need to set better standards. God, show me that You will be with me every step of the way and that when You made Your covenant of love with me, it was irrevocable. Make my dream burn within me so intensely that no sin, distraction, or desire to fit in would even compare. Amen.

Wonder Words

If you follow my decrees and are careful to obey my commands, I will send you the seasonal rains. The land will then yield its crops, and the trees of the field will produce their fruit.

—Leviticus 26: 3–4

These are the commands, decrees, and regulations that the Lord your God commanded me to teach you. You must obey them in the land you are about to enter and occupy, and you and your children and grandchildren must fear the Lord your God as long as you live. If you obey all his decrees and commands, you will enjoy a long life.

—Deuteronomy 6:1–2

It is not for kings, O Lemuel, to guzzle wine. Rulers should not crave alcohol. For if they drink, they may forget the law and not give justice to the oppressed.

—Proverbs 31:4

chapter 7

Sparkle with Queen Thoughts

> Think like a queen. A queen is not afraid to
> fail. Failure is another stepping stone to
> greatness.
>
> —*Oprah Winfrey*

In a world swarming with hurt people who hurt people, you and I have to be our own cheerleader. It's easy to let negative words or rejection affirm our feelings of self-doubt. We have to stand guard and devise an action plan to take those taunting thoughts captive and transform them into life-giving fuel.

To help control our thoughts, think of it this way: All the voices in your head fall into two categories, life/love and death/fear. Those voices are either fueling your life—including your dreams, identity, and health—or they're destroying it. Just because a thought drifts into your head doesn't mean you have to let it stay there. Negative thoughts may wander in without your conscious summoning, but you certainly don't have to let them stay there. Come on, you are stronger than that. You and I have the resurrection power of God living within us. If that power raised Jesus from the dead, it can certainly help you change your thoughts to benefit you rather than destroy you.

Proverbs 23:7 says, "As a person thinketh in his heart, so he becomes." We hear a lot about the power of positive thinking. So much sometimes that a message, sermon, or article on positive thinking goes in one ear and out the other. I'm thinking to myself, *Yep, I know that. I'm positive. Got it.* Do you ever feel like you've become immune to a message?

But *knowing* about the power of thoughts as a concept isn't enough. Only when we actually *practice* positive thoughts can we experience their life-changing benefits.

Maybe you have a dream in your heart that seems unattainable and far out of reach. It seems like it will take a lot of work, support, and resources that you don't have to make it come true. The dream may seem so daunting that you quit before you even start. Believe me, I have felt this way many times on my journey with my blog, SheIsMore.com. Beyond my online magazine, I plan to launch quarterly retreats, traveling conferences, teaching videos, Bible study series, apparel, jewelry, and inspirational resources that enhance our journeys with God. Some days, thinking of it all excites me and other days I feel completely overwhelmed. All I can see is my lack of resources, weakness in strategy development, and other women already succeeding in my dream. I feel so small, unnecessary, and common. *How could anyone possibly need what I have to give?*

Sometimes, I feel strong enough to stop the negative thoughts. But there are days I feel too weak and I buckle under the weight of them. I surrender to the oddly satisfying, downward spiral of self-hate.

Curled up in bed, I let the thoughts consume me. *I hate myself. I'm nothing special. God doesn't love me; nobody loves me. What am I doing with my life? Why am I trying?* Sound familiar?

Once I'm in this place, it takes a couple days—okay, sometimes a couple weeks—to snap back out. But when I finally do, I remind myself of the type of thinking I had on my journey to become Miss USA. Intentional thoughts filled with belief and vision.

Our dreams aren't going to happen without intense intentionality about thinking like a queen. In the years leading up to Miss USA, my family didn't have the finances to buy me a winning wardrobe or pay for my entry fees. Before pageants, I dealt with painful cystic acne and my face hurt to smile. I was the new girl at school, and to make matters worse, even my love for dance was tainted when, as a teenager, I was placed in a dance company with elementary-age girls. There I was, the uncomfortably tall high schooler who stood out awkwardly among a sea of much younger, smaller dancers. I wanted to become invisible. Looking in the mirror, I didn't see much evidence that I had what it took to become Miss USA. There didn't even seem to be evidence that I was good enough to dance with girls my own age. But I tried to focus on that inner *knowing* I'd had since I was a young girl about who I was. I tried to focus on the dreams I believe God inspired within me.

What is your inner knowing? Do you feel like a quiet voice has told you something about the good in your future or about who you truly are? It's time to listen to it.

Maybe you can relate to an experience like mine. Or maybe you will face obstacles that challenge what you believe about who you are and what you are called to do. When you experience doubt, remember you can't always control your circumstances but you *can* control your thoughts. There is power in that. See, when I was excluded from dancing with girls my own age, I would change my thoughts: *It's okay, I'm going to be Miss USA one day.* When I looked in the mirror and saw pain, ugliness, loneliness, and depression, I thought, *It's okay, I'm going to be Miss USA one day*, even if I didn't always *feel* it. You need a mantra, too. What will you say to yourself when circumstances look bleak or you endure yet another rejection? Take a moment right now to journal it.

I wanted to be a queen, so I had to think like a queen. I had to change my own thoughts. You may not want to be a queen in the sense of winning a pageant, but you *are* a queen in the spirit. You are called to be a queen in whatever your dream or goal is.

Strangely, keeping my thoughts in check actually got harder *after* I was Miss USA. Leading up to the big competition, I had always led a highly purposeful, strategic, and organized life. The structured track of school, college, and managing three jobs with extracurricular activities helped me stay focused and organized. It's what helped me think like a queen. Then, after I crowned my successor and moved to Los Angeles, I was on my own, released from the responsibility to perform or check goals off a list. The world revealed a new freedom I needed to learn to manage. It was quite daunting.

Have you ever had so much freedom, you felt aimless and a little overwhelmed?

During this new season in my life, I learned that the accomplishment of a dream doesn't end with a period. It opens borders into new territories and is punctuated with an ellipsis...

After winning Miss USA, my life swirled into a new dimension. No longer in the familiarity of my life back home, and no longer being sent the daily itineraries I received during my year as Miss USA, I found that the world truly was my oyster. But this time, there was no formula or strategy in place, no teacher or boss to manage and guide me.

How do we think like a queen when we don't know where we are headed? We get reconnected to our hearts and listen to God. We pay attention to how He is speaking and leading. Then, upon His inspiration, we decide on a new dream and trust the Lord to direct our steps. The exciting part is that you already *are* a queen in God's Kingdom, as His beloved daughter. Now, you just have to get in agreement with Him and think like it.

Here are five ways to think like a queen:

1. Agree with God.

How can two walk together, unless they be agreed?
—Amos 3:3

I love this verse so much. You can't walk with God unless you agree with Him. Just like you can't grow a business, family, or relationship where there is discord and division. Agree with what God says about you, agree upon which direction you are going, and agree with the promises He has spoken. You can't really know what those things are unless you read His word and spend time with Him. The more time you spend with God and study His word, the more quickly you can decipher thoughts that are of Him and thoughts that aren't. Thoughts from God are always life-giving, never destructive (John 6:63). He provides clarity, not confusion (1 Corinthians 14:33), and He is convicting, not condemning (John 16:8).

2. Take every thought captive.

We demolish arguments and every pretension that sets itself up against the knowledge of God, and we take captive every thought to make it obedient to Christ.
—1 Corinthians 10:5

You and I have the privilege of living in God's Kingdom and the Kingdom lives within us. But we still live in a broken world full of sin and temptation, injustice, rejection, pain, and suffering. We are in the tension between two realms. Our original and eternal home is Heaven, and our temporary home is the world.

The Bible is very clear when it calls us to be in the world, but not of it (John 17:16). This means we are made to set ourselves apart by taking a stand against Satan's shiny and deceitful schemes and filling ourselves with the light of God's delight.

Guarding against the enemy's tactics starts in the mind. Our thoughts are the first thing Satan attacks and fuels with lies. He causes us to question God, His promises, His presence, His blessings, and His truth. When a thought enters your mind that doubts God or anything of Him, acknowledge it as Satan's destructive whisper, delete it, and then replace it with the life-giving Truth. It's normal for hateful, doubtful, or negative thoughts to drift into our minds. It becomes a problem when we meditate on these thoughts and allow them to grow. We get to choose who we give power to: God or Satan.

3. Think about joy.

So a man thinketh in his heart, so he becomes.

—Proverbs 23:7

Often we hear a successful person say about their dream, "I eat, sleep, and breathe _____." It may sound all-consuming, but its impact is real. It means they thought about that goal all the time. Keeping our dream in focus motivates our actions, behavior, and discipline.

I absolutely love singing. It makes my soul come alive. I grew up singing all the time, around the house, while I was eating, doing chores, playing, anything really. I sang solos in church and community functions, so naturally I joined the chorus in school. This is when part of my joy was tainted. I auditioned for every solo for six years and never got chosen once. It hurt my feelings that my teachers kept overlooking me and chose the same girls *every* time. It also made me mad. Sometimes it's good to have a little righteous anger in you, as long as you use it as power to charge you forward.

Instead of letting my teachers steal my joy for singing, I thought, *Since they don't appreciate my voice, I'll go somewhere that does.* So when our community theater company announced they were doing *The Sound of Music* that summer, I auditioned for the role of Liesl Von Trapp. It was a dream role because I was raised on this musical's magic carried by the charming Julie Andrews. I'd get to perform the whimsical number "Sixteen Going On Seventeen" with my love interest, Rolf. It would be an incredible production in a gorgeous theater, with a full orchestra, at least twenty shows, and a packed audience every night.

I remember getting the phone call a week after my final callback for the role. I saw Opera House Theatre Company pop up on the caller ID, but I was too nervous to answer. My mama and I sat on the porch swing, holding our breath and squeezing each other's hands as we played back the voice mail that said:

"Hi, Kristen, this is Maureen with Opera House Theatre Company. I am calling to offer you the role of Liesl..."

AHHHHHH!!! I don't even know what she said after that because my mother and I let out vocal cord–stripping screams! Hot tears of overwhelming joy filled my eyes and poured down my face. I had never screamed like that before!

I had the time of my life that summer and loved every minute. To top it off, my high school chorus teacher was in the audience one night. At school the next week, he didn't compliment me or acknowledge my performance, but I didn't need him to anymore. When we are filled and focused on the joy of doing what we love, the need for affirmations lose their importance and power over you.

When you love doing something and when you really want

something, don't let the naysayers or overlookers change your queen thinking. Center your thoughts in your royal identity and use your mind to *help* you, not to *hurt* you.

Since you already are a queen, imagine yourself as that confident, empowered woman moving steadily toward her goals.

Thinking like this should impact the way you operate, especially in situations when you feel insecure or inferior. Remember, you aren't striving to become something you aren't. You are focusing on the queen you *already are* in the heavenly realms. Your original design is beautiful, pure, and inspiring. Think about the woman God made you to be *before* you were even conceived. Think about how He crafted you in your mother's womb and chose every bit of your personality and physicality to reflect His glorious image.

Think like the queen you are.

4. Remember the power of the Kingdom.

If then you have been raised with Christ, seek the things that are above, where Christ is, seated at the right hand of God. Set your minds on things that are above, not on things that are on earth.

—Colossians 3:1–2

We don't have to be ruled by what we see in the world or what makes sense logically. Life can be radically different from the way it is now if we live with the power that comes with being God's daughter and with Christ by our side. Earthly problems are flecks next to Heaven's possibilities. Our future is God's history. He's not worried so we shouldn't be either.

You are not dead, meaningless, hopeless, or lost. You are raised with Christ and called to seek the things that are above. How different would your life be if you set your mind on the Heavenly power you have access to every day? It can't just be in the morning, or when you're in a crisis, or when you hit a low. We have to reset our minds throughout the day so we can be firmly rooted when the unexpected comes our way.

Supercharge your mind-set by knowing you are supported and equipped with God's abundant storehouse of unlimited resources and riches.

5. Think about whatever is lovely.

And now, dear brothers and sisters, one final thing. Fix your thoughts on what is true, and honorable, and right, and pure, and lovely, and admirable. Think about things that are excellent and worthy of praise.
—Philippians 4:8

When Paul was teaching the believers, he couldn't let them go without a message about how to think. This verse tells us how to think and what to think on. If you think about the lyrics in the song on the radio today or the polarizing posts on your Facebook feed, those are messages that will manifest in your subconscious thoughts. In order to think like a queen, we have to monitor the messages we intake.

A daughter of God is called to think about herself, others, adversity, her dreams, her hopes, and her desires with truth and excellence. The truth is that God has plans for you to prosper and to come to no harm, plans to give you hope and a future (Jeremiah 29:11).

It's time to think like a queen. It's time to set your mind on God's truths and dwell on thoughts that are pleasing to God and productive for your life.

> *It's time to think like a queen. It's time to set your mind on God's truths and dwell on thoughts that are pleasing to God and productive for your life.*

Queen Thoughts = The Sparkle Effect

Prayer

Dear Father:

You know every one of my thoughts, and You know the dark places I tend to go. God, I confess my current thought life doesn't honor myself or You. I struggle with anxiety and depression and it's so easy to fall back into that cycle. Positive thinking hasn't worked. But Your Word will not return void because Your Word isn't just positive thoughts. Your Word is living and active and sharper than any double-edged sword. Please help me to choose Your beauty, promise, and love to meditate upon. Point me to the right Scriptures that will speak directly to me. Protect my mind with the helmet of truth and salvation. When I'm in a funk and there seems to be nothing for which to be thankful, I will be thankful for the gift of eternal life. Thank You for giving me the mind of Christ. Help me to think like the queen You made me to be so I may sparkle Your radiance in this world. Amen.

Wonder Words

It is the same with my word.
I send it out, and it always produces fruit.
It will accomplish all I want it to,
and it will prosper everywhere I send it.

—Isaiah 55:11

For the word of God is alive and powerful. It is sharper than the sharpest two-edged sword, cutting between soul and spirit, between joint and marrow. It exposes our innermost thoughts and desires.

—Hebrews 4:12

Put on salvation as your helmet, and take the sword of the Spirit, which is the word of God.

—Ephesians 6:17

Don't copy the behavior and customs of this world, but let God transform you into a new person by changing the way you think. Then you will learn to know God's will for you, which is good and pleasing and perfect.

—Romans 12:2

You will keep in perfect peace
all who trust in you,
all whose thoughts are fixed on you!

—Isaiah 26:3

chapter 8

Sparkle with Queen Speech

For beautiful eyes, look for the good in others;
for beautiful lips, speak only words of kindness;
and for poise, walk with the knowledge that
you are never alone.

—*Audrey Hepburn*

Have you ever met someone you thought was beautiful and then felt suddenly jarred out of admiration when they opened their mouth? Mmm-hmm, you know what I'm talking about. On the other hand, have you met someone you considered physically plain at first, but she grew more and more lovely as she spoke? Me, too.

Words are powerful. They are an expression of what's in our heart and mind. Do you speak with grace and integrity? Or is your speech critical and vulgar? A queen speaks in such a way that causes one to wonder why we say kind things about an unkind person.

Your words have the power to magnify your inner beauty or to diminish your outer beauty. In order to walk in your royal identity, you must speak like the queen you are called to be. Even when your circumstances say otherwise, speaking out faith-filled declarations can change *everything*. Proverbs 18:21 tells us that the power of life and death is in the tongue. That means the words we speak have the power to uplift and direct the course of our lives, feelings, and relationships. They also have the power to destroy and prevent us from the life we are intended to have. A situation you're facing may look bleak right now, but that doesn't mean you have to dwell on it and keep talking about it. You can use the power of your words to direct the change you desire.

Our lips are small but they have the power to direct our course, just like the rudder of a boat. The way we speak influences our transformation from the inside out. As the King's daughter, you and I need to make our speech truly match our royal identity. God created the world by speaking words. We are made in the image of God to imitate Him. Imagine the miracle you can create with your words, whether it's a miracle outside or a miracle inside of you.

The Bible shows us how to speak as a queen; here are the ways.

1. Decree a thing.

To decree something is to declare a thing with certainty and boldness, not with question. In Job 22:28, God says to decree a thing and it shall be established and the light will shine on all your ways. Take an assessment of how you have been talking. Speak truth with a capital T, the Truth, over yourself instead of half-truths.

When planning my wedding, I felt very stressed at first. I am not a details or logistics person. I'm a visionary and my visions tend to parallel scenes from fairy-tale books or Disney movies. In other words, my visions can be quite lavish, and my idea of a 150-guest, enchanted garden wedding with twinkling lights everywhere and chandeliers hanging from every tree was no different. My idealistic heart didn't consider the actual cost of my dream wedding. I just thought it would magically come together like it did for Cinderella, complete with a horse-drawn carriage. (I know, I sound crazy.) I was in for a harsh awakening as I started getting quotes from venues and vendors. I thought, *Who in the world would spend a salary on a wedding?* Well, apparently a lot of people, which is why they can charge inflated amounts the moment you say the word *wedding*.

I guess vendors and venues assume one of two things: that you have really wealthy parents, or you'll give into the pressure of having a Pinterest-worthy wedding.

Neither was the case for Kris and me. We were paying for the wedding and we wanted to pay in cash. How in the world was I going to have my dream wedding?

I remember crying with Kris. What do you do with a dream in your heart and limited resources to match? Do you get "realistic" in the name of practicality, to be forever rattled by the questions of *what if* or *I wish*? That option just doesn't feel right. But is it wrong or superficial to desire that dream wedding celebration?

One morning I was reading the Bible and came across this verse that stopped me right in my confusion: "He brought me to the banqueting house, and his banner over me was love" (Song of Solomon 2:4 KJV).

Oh, snap. *Yes.* I sat there in a moment of awe and clarity. God celebrates over us with a banner of love; He leads us into the banquet hall of love. He created covenant relationship and He celebrates it. Why would we not have permission to celebrate or to be celebrated lavishly? In that moment, I felt the Lord say, "Ask me to provide for you. Ask me to host your dream wedding. You are my daughter and I want you to have it."

My eyes dripped tears. My heart was wrecked. I hadn't considered asking my *Heavenly* Father to provide for my wedding. He has an unlimited treasure chest of provision and He loves me. I'm crying as I write this. Crying over how sweet, how extravagant, how uniquely loving He is. He knows my heart. He knows your heart, too. He created it. He adores it. And He fills it.

That is exactly what He did. From that day on, I decided to decree God's miraculous provision and favor over my wedding planning.

I can't tell you the amount of surprising moments we experienced with people, friends, and vendors who generously offered their resources. It was one of the most divine journeys I had walked through. Fees were waived, the floral designer gave me my $500 bouquet as a gift, the DJ offered his full services with full light display for a quarter of his normal rate, and Kris and I modeled in exchange for our engagement photos. The best, most touching part is what two of my best friends did for me.

One night, I was lying in bed and heard a knock on the door. When I opened it, there was a long box lying at my feet. I stared at it and looked to see there was no one in the hallway. I was a little scared to move. *Was something or someone going to jump out of it?* Suddenly, I heard faint giggling coming from the stairwell.

My friends Brittany and Claire emerged with their phone held up and videotaping me. I just stood there and asked them, "What is going on? What did you girls *do?*"

They exclaimed, "Open it!"

My hands were shaking and my heart was pounding. I slowly and carefully opened the box, having no idea what was inside, yet feeling it was special.

When the tissue paper fell away, I gasped and threw my hands over my face as I melted on the floor in bawling tears.

It was my wedding gown.

I wasn't going to buy one. I had decided to wear an old white pageant gown I already had. But they thought I deserved a real wedding gown. So they went to the only store where I had tried on gowns and bought the one I loved—complete with alterations and the beautiful, cathedral veil.

My heart was undone. The little holes once inflicted by loneliness were completely washed over in a wave of this act of thoughtful generosity. Brittany and Claire were beaming with excitement and I was overcome by their sincere hearts. I felt so loved in that moment.

Who knows what will happen when you decree a thing? It could be as serious as a physical healing, a restored marriage, the salvation of a loved one, a mended heart, an addiction broken, or it could be something as fun as a promotion at work, the purchasing of a dream home, or favor in an opportunity. Nothing is too big, too serious, too trivial, or superficial to God. He cares about the things you are care about. He even cares about things like getting that gown you really want for a pageant or clearing up your skin.

Who knew that decreeing something as seemingly trivial as my dream wedding would lead to more than I realized. It also led to the soothing of a childhood heartache. I didn't know or believe I could be loved or cared about by other girls the way Claire and Brittany showed me, especially on such a meaningful level. That's why we should decree a thing, because we don't know what will be established by it . . . but God always does.

2. Be silent.

Do you ever leave a girls' night or a social setting and experience the over-sharing *hangover?* What I mean is, do you feel regretful or guilty about certain things you may have said or wish you hadn't shared? I most definitely have.

It is really easy to open up and feel trusting when you are face-to-face with people. That's probably why salespeople always try to get in-person appointments. They know they can get us to give in to a sale more easily that way. In the same sense, we can give in to the betrayal of a secret, an unpleasant opinion about a friend, or sharing a thought you haven't had time to process. It is the pressure or comfort we feel in a moment that leads to overtalking. And it is, oh, so dangerous.

Many Bible verses advise us to be silent and guard our mouths with diligence. You may have heard your mama say, "There's a reason God gave you one mouth and two ears."

This sound wisdom can be drowned out by the justification of entitlement to free speech. But remember, every right comes with responsibility. A queen certainly has a right to say what she wants. She's the queen! But is it responsible for her to blurt out whatever she is thinking? Does a queen vent her negative feelings on social media after a bad day? No. She could wake up tomorrow and wish she'd never written it. The words of a queen impact others. Sure, she could recant and apologize, but the damage has already been done.

As a queen, you don't get to just spew out whatever is on your mind, especially when it isn't positive, constructive, or productive. Think of Princess Diana or Kate Middleton. A queen is wise and guards her mouth with all diligence, especially when there isn't anything good or Godly to say. Proverbs 29:11 says: "A fool gives full vent to his spirit, but a wise man quietly holds it back" (ESV). Only say today what you will stand by tomorrow.

> *A queen is wise and guards her mouth with all diligence, especially when there isn't anything good or Godly to say.*

3. Be encouraging.

I went to lunch with a beautiful friend of mine one day. She is a former beauty queen and successful model. During our lunch, she told me she was struggling with feeling beautiful. A switch flipped inside me that said, "Oh, heck no. Nope." I got all ferocious mama bear and said, "Girl, remember how God sees you. He says, 'You are altogether beautiful, my darling, there is no flaw in you.'"

At this, her eyes filled with tears and she said she had never heard that before. My friend had no idea God looked at her and called her "beautiful" and "darling." It reminded me of myself when I didn't know that either. I had forgotten for a moment that there are still women in the world, even the ones we would least expect, who don't know they are beautiful.

To make matters worse, there are Christians who literally don't know how God sees them. I used to be one of them until one hot June day in 2012. My husband, who at the time I had been dating for only three weeks, took me to a church called Bethel in Redding, California. The moment I walked in the room, girls my age flocked around me and started speaking words of inspiration, destiny, and promise over me. I'd never had girls do that for me before. I didn't even know encouragement like this was a thing. I had always been a huge complimenter, but was met with accusations that I was fake. My life was changed when these girls were saying things like, "You are powerful, you are deep, you have an anointing of Queen Esther on you." From then on, I began creating spaces where women call out the gold in one another.

Your encouragement could change someone's life, too. Why hold back the good we are thinking about someone? You never know how God could use it.

The fact that women, even women of the faith, don't know how God sees them makes me angry. It's an absolute injustice that can be changed by the words you speak over yourself and others.

You are a queen and the world needs you to be responsible with your right to free speech. You never know how you are going to change someone by the words you speak over them. Sometimes you'll receive the blessing of affirmation to learn how your words impacted someone. Many times, we truly won't know. But who cares? God knows and it's a treasure stored in Heaven you'll see later.

A queen uses her words to edify, uplift, and encourage people, including herself. Her speech is always gracious and peppered with gratitude, joy, and positivity. You can't wish and hope to be in a position of leadership if you don't speak like a leader. A queen helps others see what God has in store for them and reminds them who they truly are. A queen is gracious and applies the same principles in the words she speaks over her own life as well.

4. Be covering.

One of the biggest ways I see a change in my heart is when I hold myself back from talking about someone who hurt me. It's our nature to want other people to be on our side when we have been wronged, so we let other people know about it. But God calls us to a higher level. We have a new nature in Christ, but we have to choose to act in it for it to become our natural response.

A queen always acts in love, and love is trusting, not fearful. Because a queen trusts God, she is able to cover an offense by not talking about it (Proverbs 17:9). A gossip stirs up division and separates close friends. Sometimes this might be your goal, but it only hurts and stops you from being in union with God. Be wary of this behavior.

5. Be genuine and sincere.

Being genuine in your conversations with people is one of the must disarming, comforting qualities. The easiest way to speak with sincerity is to be connected to God's heart for others and yourself. This requires daily maintenance. When I find myself in a difficult confrontation, I pray about what to say. Sometimes I get stuck on what someone did to me and it's hard for me to move past a rehearsal of their stinging comments in my mind. If you haven't been able to move past replaying those thoughts yet, it's a good sign you are not ready for a productive conversation with that person. One day, I realized something that has helped me immensely in conflict or casual conversation. I was focusing on the by-product of my issue with the offender rather than the root of the problem in my heart. Once I change my heart toward whomever has hurt me, I can suddenly see them with more compassion and understanding. Then I am ready to have a conversation that *genuinely* conveys my hurt with peace as the sincere goal. A genuine, sincere conversation or confrontation starts with asking God to show you how He sees someone.

6. Be pure.

Some say the lowest form of humor is sarcasm, but I'd beg to differ. I'd say it's crude, perverse, and degrading talk. We are surrounded by so much vulgar talk every day that it's easy to be deceived into thinking it's acceptable. We are made for more than that. How easy it can be to forget. Why degrade yourself and others with dishonoring, immodest speech when you can be the woman who ushers in the refreshment of graciousness?

7. Be timely.

It's important to have good timing and a gentle spirit when speaking. Sometimes speaking the truth in love may come at the wrong time for someone else, causing friction. If you are meant to confront someone, the Lord will give you a peace on when to move on it. Until you get that peace, stay silent and wait for the green light.

A woman who talks like a queen attracts people to her confidence, grace, faith, and kindness. You were born to be a queen, and you have everything it takes to be a leader with your words and the way you speak.

8. Be powerful.

Speak life over yourself. Be your own cheerleader. You have the power to change the way you feel by the way you speak. Don't let the enemy be the only one talking in your ear; talk back to him!

When I'm driving in the car on the way to an audition, I speak things like, "I've already booked this job. I'm thankful for this booking as I report to set right now. Thank you, God, for Your favor that goes before me in the room."

Starting your declarations with thank-yous gets you in a winning mind-set where you are already walking in your goal rather than striving for it.

9. Have an action plan.

Create an action plan by choosing ten of your favorite Bible verses. Then make those verses personal and speak them out in the morning and any other time you need it. You can customize your plan as you go. Here are a few to get you started:

I am a victor.

"No, in all these things we are more than conquerors through him who loved us." (Romans 8:37)

I have a heavenly calling.

"Therefore, holy brothers and sisters, who share in the heavenly calling, fix your thoughts on Jesus, whom we acknowledge as our apostle and high priest." (Hebrews 3:1)

I have royalty in my veins and lead with integrity.

"But you are a chosen people, a royal priesthood, a holy nation, God's special possession, that you may declare the praises of him who called you out of darkness into his wonderful light." (1 Peter 2:9)

I am designed for good works.

"For we are God's handiwork, created in Christ Jesus to do good works, which God prepared in advance for us to do." (Ephesians 2:10)

I am a co-heir with Christ.

"Now if we are children, then we are heirs—heirs of God and co-heirs with Christ. If indeed we share in His sufferings in order that we may also share with His glory." (Romans 8:17)

Talking Like a Queen = The Sparkle Effect

Prayer

Dear Father:

Thank You for showing me the power of words by speaking the world into existence. Thank You for only speaking what You mean and meaning what You say. I can always trust that Your Word will not return void. Thank You for adopting me as Your chosen daughter and giving me the DNA to create my dream life with the words I speak. Please show me the promises I need to incorporate into my daily declarations, convict me when I am speaking words of death, and help me turn them into words of life. I want to be a leader not only around and in front of others, but all the time. I want to talk like a queen even in the mirror, when no one else is around. Help me to speak out words that agree with You even when I don't feel they are true for me yet. In Jesus' name, Amen.

Wonder Words

Whoever guards his mouth preserves his life; he who opens wide his lips comes to ruin.

—Proverbs 13:3

A soft answer turns away wrath, but a harsh word stirs up anger.

—Proverbs 15:1

Let no corrupting talk come out of your mouths, but only such as is good for building up, as fits the occasion, that it may give grace to those who hear.

—Ephesians 4:29

Let there be no filthiness nor foolish talk nor crude joking, which are out of place, but instead let there be thanksgiving.

—Ephesians 5:4

Let your speech always be gracious, seasoned with salt, so that you may know how you ought to answer each person.

—Colossians 4:6

chapter 9

Sparkle with Healing

People think I'm odd.... So I know how it feels to
be different, and I know how lonely that can be.

—Belle, from Beauty and the Beast

*(Note: In this chapter, I am not advising on clinical depression, but on
feeling depressed.)*

The pangs and immobilization of depression hit me in
high school and persisted through most of college. I was pre-
scribed my first antidepressant when I was seventeen years old.
I remember one day, I was on a walk with my mama and sister.
Suddenly the darkness loomed so heavily over me, I couldn't walk
with them anymore. I turned around and ran back to the house
with tears streaming down my face. I didn't know what triggered
it. I felt insufficient in everything I did. They were confused and
so was I.

I am what some would call a "feeler," and I felt everything.
The slightest look or sneer in my direction would shoot down my
spirits. I often felt like I carried a heavy weight inside me and felt
helpless to run from it.

The idea of being vulnerable through my teens and early twenties was too scary, so I didn't show what I was feeling on the outside. I became a pro at faking it, smiling, and masking my sadness with a lot of enthusiasm and smiles. Have you ever done this?

Many nights in college, I strategized ending my life. I Googled the easiest ways to commit suicide. I put so much pressure on myself to achieve high goals, to prove to myself and everyone that I was smart. Under the pressure, I began habits like consuming entire bags of frozen Reese's cups while studying late at night. Then, in guilt, I'd run on the elliptical for hours the next day. Still I gained twenty-five pounds.

I was on and off antidepressants for eight years. The weird part is, even with the help of antidepressants, I look back on those years and don't remember feeling joyful. I definitely experienced periods of happiness, but happiness and joy are different. Joy is a deep fulfillment that is unwavering. I don't remember having that.

God seemed far away in college. I drifted even farther from Him when I moved to New York City during my year as Miss USA and got into a serious relationship with an awesome guy—who also happened to be the one I spoke of earlier. My Jesus picture–carrying, cross-wearing, Bible-believing self actually got to a point where I questioned whether Jesus was necessary. *Why did He have to die? Why would God make His son do that? Couldn't we believe in God without the Jesus part?* It just didn't make sense to me anymore in my new, worldly, liberal-arts-university-educated, open mind. I got turned off by Christians and their annoying posts on social media. How in the world did I go from A to Z?

I grew up reading books like *I Kissed Dating GoodBye* and going to youth group retreats. I had high standards for the guys I dated, but my absolute, number one nonnegotiable was that he had to be a believer. I was very resolved about this. There was no first date with someone who wasn't. I know, it may sound a little intense, but hey—why waste your time or get your heart invested in something that isn't best for you??

The problem was, my experience had been with Christian guys who were great on paper but not Godly. I didn't like the way they made me feel. You may understand what I'm talking about through your own story.

When I met this great guy in New York City, the nonbeliever I mentioned earlier, I was really hoping things would work out.

We were texting one day and I asked him, "Are you a Christian?"

He replied, "No. Is that a deal breaker?"

I said, "We could never get married. But we can hang out."

Huh? I said what? Yes, I know. That was mistake number one. That one open door to "hang out" unfolded into that three-year relationship that ended with a tangled, mangled, broken heart. Compromise usually stems from emptiness. Think about it. If you're filled up on healthy food, you won't reach for a bag of chips. But, if you're starving, you'll pull in the first drive-through and order fries and a hamburger. As usual, you'll wish you hadn't. Not that this guy was a bag of chips, he was actually amazing. And it confused me.

I fell in love. His whole family was loving, warm, and had great integrity. How could I rectify that? It made me question what I thought I knew about my beliefs.

Love is about compromise, right? I wanted to make it work with my boyfriend, so I drew farther from my faith. I didn't spend as much time with God, didn't go to church regularly, didn't read the Bible, and barely prayed unless I needed or wanted something. I was still on antidepressants and the hole I felt was widening.

But the Lord has a way of wooing His daughters back to Him

when we stray too far or long. He'd much rather have us come back on our own, but He will intervene if necessary.

It was a few days before Christmas and I had just gotten home to be with my family. The first night, I was lying in bed with my sister Julia. I opened my laptop to find that my boyfriend's Facebook account was still up.

In one defining moment on a cold day in December, I read a conversation that shook me from my settledness. A clarity came over my eyes. He wasn't planning on marrying me. I felt punched in the stomach and stone-cold sobered up. Reality came crashing in; I'd been living in a fog, disillusioned by a false hope, and had compromised my faith and *who I was.*

In that moment, a fresh resolve took root in my heart. What had I been doing? Why did I think I knew better than God? Who was I to make my own rules—to only invite God into the parts of my life I didn't want to change? I realized how deceitful and destructive my own ways are. Sometimes our own ways can lead to feelings of depression.

I dug my heels in and claimed, "I'm pursuing God like I never have before. I have a lot of questions and I need more understanding, but I don't care how long it takes, I just want back into His arms." I realized I was empty without Him.

I shared all of that to say, when we drift away from God, life might go well on the outside for a time, but an emptiness will remain and grow within.

I called a girlfriend of mine, who used to irritate me with her Christian lingo and seemingly radical devoutness. But then I needed it. I asked her to come over every week and go through the Bible with me. She and I, with our friend Claire, hunkered at my tiny dining room table eating frozen yogurt and studying the Bible together. I remember drilling Brittany with questions, and she was so patient with me.

I was still on antidepressants, but one night we talked about how God's presence lives within us and it grows when we nurture it. I decided I wanted to see what would happen if I fully let go and trusted God to replace my antidepressant with His joy.

As Nehemiah tells us, "The joy of the LORD is your strength" (8:10 NIV). I wanted to know what that meant for me!

For seven years since then, I have been healed and set free of my dependency on antidepressants.

My life is so different now.

As I write this, I am overcome with a deep thankfulness for how sweet and redeeming God is. I am filled with joy to the fullest. I am sensitive to the Spirit; I know He always had my back even when I turned mine to Him. I look back on my life, I see He's never left me... not once (James 4:8).

He hasn't left you either. He has always been there. He says that when you draw near to Him, He will draw near to you. All it takes is simply turning back to Him and He will be right there with you.

Now, just to be clear, I wasn't inspired to share this because I feel joyful and happy all the time. As a matter of fact, I'm feeling down and discouraged at this moment, and I feel the need to dive into the light of God's truth and to remember how He's always been there for me.

I want to be honest because having a relationship with God doesn't mean your life will be perfect or you will always feel peaceful. But leaning on God's strength does mean that you can have the faith that He always works out everything together for your good, even when it feels like it's taking forever and doesn't make sense.

When we are walking with God, we can go boldly to the throne with life's trials and our wounds, and the Lord will respond in one way or another.

A daughter of God doesn't let feelings of depression keep her down or dull her sparkle. You are made to radiate God's light. Here is how to deal with that empty feeling when it comes creeping in:

1. Recognize spiritual warfare.

Recognize that demonic activity and attacks from the enemy are real. The devil's primary goal is to destroy you, but you have been given the authority to trample over snakes and scorpions and the forces from the dark world. Claiming the name of Jesus and praying for protection from the devil's schemes are powerful (Ephesians 6:12, Luke 10:19). Also, pray that God will break you free from feeling depressed, especially in instances where depression runs in your family. God is a healer, and He heals chemical imbalances, too.

2. Ask why it bothers you.

If there is someone or something bringing out the worst in you, rather than putting the blame on them, step back and ask yourself *why?* Be honest with yourself and get to the root of it by asking why something hurts you. Is it a brokenness within you that needs healing? Where did this wound come from? Was it a defining moment in your past that made you start believing negative things about yourself? Maybe it was a moment of not measuring up or making the team that caused you to experience disappointment on a more extreme level. The Lord will reveal it to you. Discovering where a trigger originates will expose the power it has and allow you to uproot it, present the wounding to God, and pray for healing (Luke 8:17).

3. Surrender it to God.

Give your pain to God. We can be control freaks and fall into patterns of self-harm with things like eating disorders, cutting, alcohol, exercise, sugar, self-hate and so forth, in our attempt to feel some sort of control on outside pain. But when we trust God with our mind, heart, and spirit, He will lead us on a path of true and beautiful restoration (Luke 10:27). Take a moment right now to close your eyes and imagine your pain and the thing causing it. Then imagine handing it over to God. Finally, ask Him what He has for you instead. This is something you may have to do daily or even several times a day.

4. Read the Word.

I love the Word of God. It's fresh, relevant, and life-changing. The Bible is the only book filled with living and active God-breathed words that sift between our feelings and the Truth. When I am feeling anxious or worried, reading the Word is like taking a spiritual Xanax. I immediately feel calm and comforted (John 6:63). I encourage you to start with the book of Psalms if you have felt overwhelmed reading the Bible in the past. It's great encouragement that reveals the heart of God when you are feeling depressed.

5. Sing worship songs.

Shifting our minds onto the wonder, magnificence, and sweetness of God changes everything (Ephesians 5:19). Getting out of our thoughts by making a joyful noise and singing lyrics of hope and encouragement resets a downward spiral without having to force something we don't feel. Make a playlist of your favorite worship music. Some artists you might love are Kari Jobe, Steffany Gretzinger, Nicole Nordeman, Bethel, and Hillsong.

6. Be purposeful.

One of my mentors said people who feel depressed often sense a lack of purpose. Our lives are meant to be meaningful, and if we aren't living that out, it's only natural that emptiness would creep in. Even if you don't know what your purpose is, see what you can do for someone else. Sometimes, when I'm feeling depressed, I'll use it as a reminder to reach out to someone else. I send a text or voice note asking how they are and how I can pray for them. It's amazing how connecting with a friend, hearing their struggle, and praying for them helps me. Many times, the heaviness inside me tangibly lifts.

I am not discounting the need for antidepressant medication. I do think it is helpful and even crucial in some cases. What I am saying is this: Drawing near to God can transform our lives and give us the powerful resources to help us get through our dark times.

> *Drawing near to God can transform our lives and give us the powerful resources to help us get through our dark times.*

Our true identity isn't rooted in our hardship, diagnosis, relationship status, mistakes, disappointments, or what we do or don't achieve. Your identity is God's chosen daughter, which makes you royalty whether you feel it or not.

Receiving God's Healing = The Sparkle Effect

Prayer

Dear Father:

You care about my life; You care about how I feel. Father, I hate when depression sets in, and I don't want it to rule my life. I want You to rule my life. God, You came to give me life in abundance, so please invade my heart and draw close to me when I come to You in prayer. Will You please let me feel You? I declare in the name of Jesus that I am set free from depression! I have inherited joy because You are my strength. Amen.

Wonder Words

When the cares of my heart are many, your consolations cheer my soul.

—Psalm 94:19

Anxiety in a man's heart weighs him down, but a good word makes him glad.

—Proverbs 12:25

Likewise the Spirit helps us in our weakness. For we do not know what to pray for as we ought, but the Spirit himself intercedes for us with groanings too deep for words.

—Romans 8:26

And the prayer of faith will save the one who is sick, and the Lord will raise him up. And if he has committed sins, he will be forgiven.

—James 5:15

chapter 10

Sparkle with Childlike Wonder

If I go, there's just no telling how far I'll go.

—*Moana*

My husband says one of the reasons he fell in love with me was my wonder for life. He loves that I twirl and spin around in the grocery store aisle. I laugh loud and hard at the cheesiest jokes and get giddy over twinkling lights and sunsets. I never noticed these things about myself until he pointed them out.

"That is what we should be like as Christians," he said. "Full of wonder because we always have hope available to us."

Life throws us curveballs, loss, massive disappointments, and grief. People we love the most let us down in the worst ways and our hearts get broken. How in the world do we maintain a starry-eyed wonder and childlike excitement?

Jesus is clear when He says, "Anyone who will not receive the Kingdom of God like a little child will never enter it" (Mark 10:15 NIV). Childlike wonder is important to maintain.

Think back to when you were seven years old. Let's say you really loved dolls and your grandmother said to you, "Darling, I am giving you all the American Girl dolls, the book collections, and all the doll clothes so you can change their outfits, with a huge dollhouse for them to live in." You would throw your arms around your grandmother and shriek with excitement! You wanted only one doll—maybe two, if you were really good—but she is giving you more than you would have asked for or even imagined! You wouldn't think twice about whether you deserved all this or not. You wouldn't say, "Oh, Grandmother, I can't accept this. I wasn't nice to my brother this week." That's the childlike wonder you must have about the gifts of your Heavenly Father. Jesus says we will not receive the Kingdom of Heaven unless we become like little children. Little children are wide-eyed and pure-hearted, believe in gorgeous possibilities, and receive gifts wholeheartedly and enthusiastically.

Maybe a part of our wonder starts to die when we realize Santa isn't real, or when a parent abandons us, or when we were lied to for the first time. As we grow older, we experience harsh realities in this world that were never a part of God's design for us. The wonder and hope God placed in our hearts begin to wrestle with the tension between our home in Heaven and our home on the earth. That's when we have a choice to make. We can choose to hope for Kingdom possibilities.

Another reason we can lose our wonder is that it feels too risky to believe and dream. Especially if believing and dreaming has let us down or severely humiliated us before. I'll be honest, I was severely humiliated when I wasn't allowed to be in dance class with girls my own age. I tried to keep going with the hope I might advance, but I eventually couldn't do it anymore. I took myself out of it. Have you ever not tried out for something because you might not get picked? It can feel safer to take ourselves out so no one else has to. Do you ever feel guilty for being happy? Do you find yourself waiting for the other shoe to drop, so to speak? Do you give up before you even start? These are things we do to protect ourselves from the letdown we've experienced after hoping.

Sometimes, we aren't even aware of how events or people have damaged our wonder. We may subconsciously suppress heartbreak or hurt, but no matter how much we stuff it down, it manages to steal our child-like wonder. The symptoms of old wounds can manifest themselves in different expressions when they are triggered. For instance, has someone ever made a lighthearted comment that actually shot straight to your heart? That could be evidence of a trigger for you. A trigger is something that indicates we have underlying, unhealed trauma or pain and it just got touched on. It's powerful to recognize your triggers because they will help you identify the point of pain you may need to work through.

I didn't realize I had any old wounds until Kris and I started premarital counseling. It was then that I became aware of my own "triggers." For example, a trigger for me is when Kris walks out of the room during an argument. It triggers feelings of being too much or not enough. These triggers reveal unhealed wounds from being forgotten, overlooked, or walked out on.

Kris and I went to our church marriage retreat at a beautiful hotel in Laguna Beach. While we were there, the speakers talked about a relationship boot camp they led. They invited us to go. It would take place two weeks before our wedding, and we decided it would be fun! But we didn't realize what we were getting ourselves into. The boot camp was full of couples married for ten or more years, some with divorce papers on the table. They all seemed miserable. None of the couples even cared to sit together.

The boot camp was intense with strict rules. No coffee, gum, candy, ibuprofen, sodas, phones, or anything that could be a distraction or comfort. The instructors led us through role-playing exercises, and people were crying and experiencing break-throughs left and right.

Kris and I were passing all the exercises with flying colors. Many of the couples were pretty annoyed with our in-love-ness and public display of affection. They kept saying things like, "Oh, you won't be there long; we used to be in love just like you."

I wondered if we would have a moment of tension, too.

On the last day of boot camp, we played this "game" called Lifeline. We were asked to imagine that we were sinking on the *Titanic*. We stood in a big circle and each of us got three ropes we could use to save three people. We needed to choose wisely how we would use our ropes. One by one, we went around the circle and stood in front of one person at a time. They would hold out their hand and beg, "Do you have a lifeline for me?" Our response could only be: "Yes, I have a lifeline for you," or "No, I don't have a lifeline for you." You had to look the person in their eyes when you said it.

Obviously, I would save Kris and two other people. By this point in the weekend, we had heard people's stories, cried together, and felt compassion for one another. It was harder than I thought to look someone in the eyes and tell them I was choosing not to save them. It was also hard to be looked in the eye and be told they were choosing not to save me. One by one, people looked me in the eye and said, "No, I don't have a lifeline for you." But it was okay; Kris would have one saved for me. I had already saved him with one of my lifelines. It was easy. You just make a decision to save your partner and then do it...right?

I was anxiously waiting for Kris to get close and stand in front of me. Finally, there he was. *Yay, now you can be my knight in shining armor and rescue me!* He looked me in the eyes as I held out my hand and asked somewhat flirtatiously, "Do you have a lifeline for me?" He looked down at his feet and didn't answer me.

What's going on? I thought. *Is he okay?*

He started tearing up. My mind was racing, I was so confused.

The facilitator made me ask him again. "Do you have a lifeline for me?"

He still wouldn't look at me until the facilitator said, "We have to keep it moving. Look her in the eyes and answer."

He finally looked at me and said, "No, I don't have a lifeline for you."

Have you ever been so shocked by something that you have a super delayed reaction? That's what happened. All kinds of thoughts were swirling through my mind. *Maybe he knows something about this Lifeline game I don't. I'm sure there's a good explanation. It's okay; it's just a game. It's just a game. How hard is it to save a rope for me? Why did he forget me? I'm sure he didn't mean to. He always chooses other people first. I can't do this. I don't think we can get married. I don't want to be forgotten. If he brushes this off, we are done.*

When the exercise was over, we all sat back in our chairs in the circle. He was across the room from me. I could feel him looking at me, but I couldn't look at him. My initial shock had settled and all I could do was stare at the floor.

Finally, our break started and he made a beeline to me and got on his knees.

He said, "I'm so sorry, baby. I'm so sorry. Now I see for myself that you haven't been getting the best of me. This scared me. I get distracted by everyone else's needs and then you get my scraps. But you deserve the best of me. From now on, I will choose you first and make you my priority."

Honestly, if he had responded any differently, I don't think we would have gotten married two weeks later. It was a huge breakthrough moment for both of us. We both learned that being overlooked is a trigger for me because it reinforces past hurts.

Kris realized that he overextends himself feeling he needs to be everything to everyone.

Knowing these things about ourselves gives us the power to handle conflict better in our relationship. If we are in an argument, we've established that Kris doesn't leave the room because that triggers feelings of abandonment in me. When Kris is late or forgets something I said, I am able to give grace because I know he tends to overextend himself and it isn't personal.

When we have unidentified wounds, we can get caught up in a pattern of hurting others and ourselves without meaning to. The hope is that we are offered a whole life with a whole heart in Jesus. If you will be brave enough to connect with your heart and ask God to help you see your points of pain, He will begin to show you how it has been limiting hope and wonder in areas of your life. When you are connected to your heart and let go of any shame attached to the pain, you can begin to connect with others in healing, magical ways.

You can smile as big as you want, have your makeup done perfectly, have the hottest body, and rock stylish outfits. But the sparkle in your eye and warmth in your presence will be missing when you lose your wonder. That is why it is so important to give your hurt over to the Lord. Releasing hurt and choosing hope will allow you to radiate with childlike wonder.

Even though the main source of my hurt was girls and older women, some even in the church, my heart still hopes for girls to be secure in their true identity. That hope led me to form a women's group in LA full of gorgeous hearts. My heart is full of excitement to see these amazing young women coming together with a common vision to bring transformation to other young women. We've produced retreats and conferences that share what we do in group with more girls! None of this would happen if I let hurtful people diminish my wonder. Hope sees what currently is and then asks the question, "What could be?"

When your hope is in Christ, you can have hope for Kingdom possibility in this life. I wonder what God wants you to hope for? What is the main source of your hurt? He can empower you to use your pain for a greater purpose. The choice is yours. Will you use your suffering as a weapon to shut people out or will you wear it as a crown to show compassion? That is the power of choice combined with the power of God.

Take a moment to reflect and ask yourself, "How can God use my pain for a message of hope? Where can I find wonder in the midst of suffering?"

The Kingdom of God lives within us. But we have to cultivate the space to receive and experience it.

Just like a seed that can't grow in rocky, unwatered soil, the Kingdom can't grow within us when our hearts are hard and calloused.

How do we maintain that childlike wonder when we endure so much heartbreak?

Here are ten ways I've found to be helpful:

1. Understand who God is.

1 John 4:18 says, "Perfect love drives out fear" (NIV). God is perfect love; He is whole and complete. We allow our hearts to become hardened out of fear, but God casts out fear and replaces it with love. No matter how much hurt we go through, He will always mend our hearts back up. Let Him knit your heart back to wholeness and trust that He will bring every good work to a full completion (Psalm 47:3 and Philippians 1:6).

2. Don't generalize.

Just because one boy—or even a lot of boys—broke your heart or cheated on you doesn't mean all boys are bad. Just because you never had genuine friendships with girls for most of your life doesn't mean you can't now or in the future. You may need to re-evaluate the type of people you've been letting in, but great people are out there with whom you can absolutely have beautiful friendships. Ask God to bring wonderful people into your life and to help you navigate the waters of relationship dynamics with wisdom.

3. Embrace your story.

One of the biggest things that helped me maintain wonder through the midst of rejection from my younger years was reading inspirational biographies. Everyone who ever achieved happiness or anything great overcame adversity first. Maybe you are like me and don't even know if you have a story. Trust me, you do and it matters. Maybe you don't think you have gone through anything hard enough to qualify for a testimony. Or maybe something so awful has happened in your life, you have suppressed it and vowed never to unlock it or talk about it. Your story connects you to other people and even yourself in a more loving way. Have a meeting with yourself, get out your journal and pen, and ask the Lord to guide your memory and your thoughts as you write out the story of your life. I created *Rise Up with God: The Guided Journal* to help lead in this as well. It's available on Amazon.com.

4. Take time to notice God's splendor.

Sometimes when I'm stuck in Los Angeles' crazy five-o'clock traffic, feeling the stress of the day, I look out at the sky and focus on the beaming hues in the sunset. God romances us every day with His paintings in the sky, the glittering stars at night, and the flowers that bloom around us. When everything else is a mess, we always have that. When we stop to notice, He meets us there and allows us to witness things we didn't see before. That is wonder. By God's spoken word, the heavens came into being and the earth was formed out of water. Where is He showing you His splendor in your life? (2 Peter 3:5).

5. Be thankful for where God has brought you.

God can bring you out of more situations than the devil can lead you into. He also works behind the scenes for us in ways we don't even realize. Ask God to show you some of those moments. It may be preventing a car accident, restoring a relationship, or letting you pass a test by one point. My favorite author, Joyce Meyer, always says, "You may not be where you want to be, but thank God you aren't where you used to be." "He drew me up from the pit of destruction, out of the miry bog, and set my feet upon a rock, making my steps secure" (Psalm 40:2 ESV).

6. Fan the flame in your heart with worship.

Worship is the place where God meets me the most powerfully. Hearing God's voice is more likely in worship because we are seeking His face and His presence, instead of His hand and what He can give us. Worship is magical whether you are in church, a worship concert, or alone on your living room floor listening to your favorite worship album. I love the Kari Jobe album, *The Garden.*

As the prophet Isaiah put it, "Lord, you are my God; I will exalt you and praise your name, for in perfect faithfulness you have done wonderful things, things planned long ago" (Isaiah 25:1 NIV).

Isn't that so fun to think about? God will do the wonderful things for you He has already planned!

7. Receive.

Having Godly boundaries is letting the good in and the bad out. The writer of Proverbs says to guard your heart above all else, because it determines the course of your life (4:23). Many people confuse this verse by blocking their heart from receiving good experiences and connections with people.

Christian psychologist and author Dr. Henry Cloud describes it like this: Imagine your heart has a fence with a door. The fence is the protector that keeps the good in, and the door opens to let more good in and to let the bad out. Receive blessings, but be discerning with the treasure of your heart.

In the same way, Matthew 7:6 says not to cast your pearls among pigs because they will trample over them and then turn to tear you to pieces. This means that you can't give your heart to people who are unable to see your worth.

I'll expand on this in the chapter on Boundaries.

8. Wear a flowy dress and twirl.

Did you play dress-up as a young girl? Maybe you imagined all kinds of stories about who you might be or what world you lived in. I dressed up all the time and loved twirling around like a princess. Tap back into your little girly self and throw on a tutu or a fabulous, over the top outfit with lots of jewelry. Sometimes, I tap into my child-like wonder by donning a flowy dress and finding somewhere to just twirl. Well, let's be honest I do this a lot anyways. It's important to nurture that softness because it sparks our imagination, our carefreeness and creativity. Dressing up also nourishes your femininity, which opens your heart to compassion, gentleness, and connection. "But we were gentle among you, like a nursing mother taking care of her own children" (1 Thessalonians 2:7 ESV).

9. See every day as an adventure.

God loves to play with us. It often feels like a game of hide-and-seek with Him. He longs for us to seek after Him and be found. Just talk to Him like you would a friend and ask Him to reveal himself in sweet, little ways throughout the day. Praying very specifically for how you want to experience Him is the best because then it's more exciting and undeniable when He shows up to meet those specific prayers. For instance, the other day I was walking to Starbucks and I asked God to please reserve the table near the window so I could have an outside view. I had the baby with me. When I got there, it was the only table open! It was such a little thing, but so revealing of God's heart for how He enjoys being in fun, intimate relationship with us.

You can also ask Him to speak to you about something specific. For instance, I was praying about a scary situation where I didn't know what the outcome would be. Then I started noticing Scriptures, devotionals, or conversations popping up that all spoke to God's grace and deliverance from our enemies. Sure enough the result to that scary situation had God's grace all over it. When we seek Him, we will find Him. Have fun exploring how God wants to reveal Himself to you. "It is the glory of God to conceal a matter, but the glory of kings is to search out a matter" (Proverbs 25:2 NKJV).

10. Laugh more.

Laughter really is the best medicine. It's also important to note what we are laughing at. Fun, wholesome good humor is good for our soul. When we are jaded, it's easier to laugh at crudeness or distastefulness. Those sentiments only feed our bitterness. Laugh at good humor. "Then our mouth was filled with laughter, and our tongue with shouts of joy; then they said among the nations, 'The Lord has done great things for them'" (Psalm 126:2 ESV).

Life can be beautiful; it just depends on which lens we are looking through. We all have a little girl in us who wants to play, leap around, and radiate the wonders of God. That little girl just needs to be loved and tenderly cared for. Today, you can give her the love and encouragement she needed all those times she was over-looked and misused. Ask the little girl inside you, "What do you need?"

When you have childlike wonder, you won't be able to contain the sparkle in your eyes. It will radiate.

> *We all have a little girl in us who wants to play, leap around, and radiate the wonders of God.*

Childlike Wonder = The Sparkle Effect

Prayer

Dear Father:

I praise Your name because You have never left my inner child! I confess that my heart has been wounded and I have put walls up to protect it. People try to love me well, but I have rejected that love instead of receiving it openly and have hurt others in the process. God, I want to receive Your perfect love that casts out all fear. I want to receive all the power and glory and wonder of Your Kingdom that is available to me! I know I haven't been living life as fully and wondrously as Your Kingdom gives me the privilege to.

Lord, will You please show me the walls I need to tear down and grant me the wisdom to know with whom I am safe to be vulnerable? I know that You are the only one I can completely trust and that people will inevitably let me down no matter how awesome they are. But help me to know the difference between a safe, loving person letting me down and an unsafe, boundary-less person. Help me not to avoid love; I want to receive it. God, I trust You. Help me to become like a little child, full of wonder and openness to miracles.

I don't want to wait to get to Heaven to experience You; I want to usher in and dwell in the majesty of Your Kingdom while I'm here on earth. I declare that right now You are doing a work on my heart, restoring me back to softness. Your Kingdom is within me! Amen.

Wonder Words

---

*You have taught children and infants
to tell of your strength,
silencing your enemies
and all who oppose you.*

—Psalm 8:2

*Instead, I have calmed and quieted myself, like a weaned
child who no longer cries for its mother's milk. Yes, like
a weaned child is my soul.*

—Psalm 131:2

*They asked Jesus, "Do you hear what these children are
saying?" "Yes," Jesus replied. "Haven't you ever read the
Scriptures? For they say, 'You have taught children and
infants to give you praise.'"*

—Matthew 21:16

*Like newborn babies, you must crave pure spiritual milk
so that you will grow into a full experience of salvation.
Cry out for this nourishment, now that you have had a
taste of the Lord's kindness.*

—1 Peter 2:2

chapter 11

Sparkle with Rising

Just because it's what's done doesn't mean it's
what should be done.

—*Cinderella*

Some people see God as a nice add-on to their life. They think being a Christian is going to enhance their life and career, and further their goals, while also allowing them to live how they want to.

But this is not the case for a daughter of the King. Jesus didn't die on the cross so we could pick and choose where we let Him in our life. He didn't suffer so God could be our genie, granting wishes. Ultimately, Jesus came to cover the cost of our sins and to give us a home in Heaven. But that doesn't mean we have to wait until we get to Heaven to experience fullness. You can be full of Heaven now! Jesus came to set us free from all the stuff we think is protecting or promoting us. He came to set us free from the masks we wear, the pressure to compromise, and the need to be liked. Jesus gives us the confidence to choose the best path, rather than a path that feels good in the moment.

Life with God is so much more than an add-on. Life with God

shows us who we really are. Who you really are is so much better than a persona you put out into the world. Take an honest assessment of the things that are preventing you from walking in your true identity. Is it the fun you have leading guys on, an unhealthy relationship, alcohol, an eating disorder, negative self-talk, scrolling on social media, letting others control you, sexting, hook-up apps, a wrong group of friends, pretending everything is okay, saying *yes* when you want to say *no?* Or maybe you are mad at God about something. Maybe you feel He's let you down in some way and that's why you're still holding on to parts of your life that you know deep down aren't the best. I get that and it's normal. We'll talk about it more throughout the book.

In our fear or mistrust, we want to hold on to what is comfortable, and then test the waters with Jesus. But nothing wondrous happens in comfort. When Jesus called His first disciples, who were fishermen by trade, He told them to "cast down their nets and follow Him." He was asking them to exchange their former lives for what He had for them. That is a very big ask! This lifestyle was all they ever knew. It would be completely normal if they had a few questions first. But they didn't even question Him. They didn't question themselves in whether they were worthy of the call either. They immediately put down what they were doing and followed Him. That is when they became who they were made to be, "fishers of men." God used their vocation to prepare them to be disciples of nations. They stepped out of their current situation to step into the calling God had for them. What do you think God is calling you to step out of?

I have learned this verse to be powerful when you experience it for yourself: "If you try to hang on to your life, you will lose it. But if you give up your life for my sake, you will find it" (Matthew 16:25 NLT). In the live action movie *Cinderella*, Ella loses her identity when her stepmother treats her and repeatedly tells her she will never be anything but a servant girl. When she meets the prince who she believes is an apprentice, she doesn't tell him her name when he asks. Then, when she goes to the ball and realizes he is the prince, he asks her name again. She still doesn't tell him. Finally, when the king's royal guard announces that the prince is searching for the girl who lost her slipper, Ella is standing right there. But she doesn't make herself known. She doesn't rise up to the call because she is afraid she will be rejected if they find out she doesn't meet the qualifications to marry a prince. In the end, the prince spares no effort in finding her. When he does and the glass slipper fits, she asks, "will you take me as I am?" Of course, we all know he is madly in love with her and wouldn't have her any other way. The Prince of Peace pursues you, too. He takes you as you are and leads you into who you were made to be.

Thankfully, with Jesus, we can cast down our masks and comforts any day and find our true, free life in Him. It's time to start making choices that lead us closer to God—decisions that lead us down a path under His wings, and most of all, into the freedom to step into our true, royal identity.

You may really want to hear God, but what voices are you tuning into regularly? Maybe it's the inner voice of how you feel around your peers, maybe it's memories of things you regret, maybe it's the audible voices of people who criticize you. If you want a meaningful, magical life, it's time to go all in and open your ears to God and shut them to anything that affirms a negative belief about yourself. You are a queen so you can make choices that are pure, though not always popular amidst the voices.

What choices are you making right now? Do they reflect the radiance of your true identity? You are worthy to rise; you don't have to compromise.

God has a promise for you, a vision and a plan for your future.

He is just waiting for you to return to Him. I believed God had plans for me since I was a young girl. I started making tough choices as a teenager that often left me feeling isolated. Even in the pain and loneliness, preparing for the promise was more important than compromising my dream.

> *God has a promise for you, a vision and a plan for your future.*

If you want your dream to come true, you have to start living like you believe. What if your dream fell in your lap right now? Would your character and skill set match the calling?

Let's go back to the story of Cinderella. She was chosen to be royalty by the prince because she was kind and courageous. She was ready to be an example, a role model for other women of what God's redemption looks like. She was ready for the position of leadership when it came knocking at her door. Her stepsisters, Drizella and Anastasia, on the other hand, wanted position and status so badly that they hurt other people trying to get there. All that competing and striving made them uglier and uglier. If the prince had chosen one of them, they wouldn't have been ready for a position of leadership because their desire for position was leading them.

You are more than your need to be accepted by either fitting in or by gaining status. You are more than someone who lives in a life-sucking cycle of people-pleasing and compromising. People-pleasing always hurts you more than it helps you. God-pleasing always helps you even when people don't agree. You are called to positively impact people, not live to please them.

Believe what God has spoken over your life and start preparing for it. Clean out the cobwebs, get rid of the negativity, reset your mind on heavenly things, surround yourself with people you want to be like, and clean up your social media. Say *no* to disrespect and *yes* to standards. Say *yes* to choosing to live your life worthy of your incredibly important calling (Ephesians 4:1).

Deciding to Rise = The Sparkle Effect

Prayer

Dear Father:

For too long, I have wandered around aimlessly letting people control my life. God, please take away my desire to be accepted, especially by the wrong people. Lord, I pray that You will open my eyes to see the true intentions of those with whom I've been surrounding myself. Show me that I don't have to settle for less than what You would have for me and I don't have to try to impress anyone. I want to live a life that is worthy of the calling You have given me, I want to be on fire for You; I want to cast my nets down and follow You.

Jesus, I can't be a light, and I can't radiate Your love and sparkle, when I am lukewarm, halfway in, doing what I want whenever I feel like it. You have a plan for my life and I want to follow it. Help me to develop a plan for my life that is beautiful. Help me to believe in the beauty of my dreams so strongly that I always want to make the best choices that are pleasing in Your sight. In Jesus' powerful name, Amen!

Wonder Words

The Lord your God will make you abundantly prosperous in all the work of your hand, in the fruit of your womb and in the fruit of your cattle and in the fruit of your ground. For the Lord will again take delight in prospering you, as he took delight in your fathers, when you obey the voice of the Lord your God, to keep his commandments and his statutes that are written in this Book of the Law, when you turn to the Lord your God with all your heart and with all your soul.

—Deuteronomy 30:9–10

Enter by the narrow gate. For the gate is wide and the way is easy that leads to destruction, and those who enter by it are many. For the gate is narrow and the way is hard that leads to life, and those who find it are few.

—Matthew 7:13–14

Do not be deceived: God is not mocked, for whatever one sows, that will he also reap. For the one who sows to his own flesh will from the flesh reap corruption, but the one who sows to the Spirit will from the Spirit reap eternal life.

—Galatians 6:7–8

As a prisoner for the Lord, then, I urge you to live a life worthy of the calling you have received.

—Ephesians 4:1

chapter 12

Sparkle with Confidence

> You gain strength, courage, and confidence by
> every experience in which you really stop to
> look fear in the face. You are able to say to
> yourself, "I lived through this horror. I can take
> the next thing that comes along."
>
> —*Eleanor Roosevelt*

Los Angeles is the city of dreams, but it can also be the city of insecurities. Any city can breed insecurities, but for me, moving to LA even after being Miss USA caused me to question my purpose, my work ethic, my motivation, and my worth. Later, I realized it seemed to be a common sentiment among most everyone here. A life of busyness was only leading to emptiness.

I remember when I first started dating Kris, he invited me to parties, events, and gatherings with his friends. I would dread walking in because I didn't feel like I measured up to the level of successes in the room. I wanted Kris to be proud of me. I wanted to have my own thing to be proud of. I was afraid he would lose interest in me because I wasn't "hustling and grinding" as much as other beautiful young women in our social group. Do you ever feel like you're not living up to the pressure to be and do it all? I certainly did and still do sometimes!

I thought, *I might as well end this relationship before he does. I might as well show him and explain all the reasons he shouldn't want to be with me and beat him to it.*

As we've talked about before, self-sabotage occurs when we take ourselves out before anyone or anything else can. We believe we will eventually be rejected, so we reject ourselves to avoid being rejected. The interesting thing is, I knew about my royal identity at that point. But during that time, knowing that almost made me feel worse because I wasn't producing the fruit I felt should reflect my identity.

In the process of stepping into our true identity, there are always deeper levels of growth to go through. With every season, there are new layers of our identity to unveil, heal, and understand. One season of clarity and peace doesn't mean we have everything figured out for the next season. Thankfully, Kris was unmoved by my self-doubting resistance. He was steadfast and gentle. I remember one conversation over the phone when he said, "You might feel this way about yourself, but that isn't how God sees you. I see the destiny God has put in you."

I'm thinking, *How are you not running for the hills right now? Why are you willing to ride out this journey of my unforeseen destiny with me? Maybe I'll never measure up to anything great.*

Kris could have been with any high-producing, wealthy, influential woman he wanted, but he was choosing me. He said, "I don't love you because of what you can bring to the table or because of what you do. I love you because of your heart."

This is what Jesus says to us, too. He doesn't look at our outward qualities; He looks at our heart. And in case you don't think you have a good one, remember you have been given a new heart, that of a princess. Our Prince of Peace has all the power in the world. He is famous—the Holy Bible is the bestselling book in history—and yet He chooses you.

God chooses you every time. He chooses you when you are curled up on the bathroom floor crying because you feel hopeless. He chooses you when you are self-destructive. God chooses you when you try to sabotage yourself from receiving the love you have longed and prayed for. When our confidence is rooted in anything other than Christ, our lives will be one, big, hot mess anytime something goes awry.

Confidence is somewhat of a vague concept and can mislead us into the lie that *acting* confidently means we *are* confident. But that isn't always true. We have the ability to truly *be* confident rather than simply appearing confident. I've studied confidence throughout the years, and I'm amazed by the unwavering gift of confidence we've inherited as God's daughters. I'm also amazed at how long I didn't know about it. I wish I had known in my teenage years and early twenties what I know now.

Can you imagine what your life would be like if every fiber of you emanated steadfast confidence *no matter what?* It is a hard thing to imagine. A lack of confidence usually comes from being too focused on ourselves and caring too much about what others think about us.

Jesus is the best person to look at for an example of the kind of confidence we are made to have. He also shows us the power we have as the King's daughter by the way He lived as God's Son. Jesus was able to be so free and confident because His focus was on God, not Himself. We are called to be Christlike so let's take a look at what that looks like.

Confidence in Christ

I have an inheritance in Christ that trumps the temporary trappings of this world. You can be confident in taking a leap of faith and doing what the Lord calls you to do even when you don't feel confident. The Lord has deposited the Holy Spirit within you that seals the gift of heavenly citizenship. That means you already have a slice of Heaven within you now that you can tap into (Ephesians 1:13–14).

I never have to strive on my own. My adequacy and sufficiency always come from Christ alone. It's amazing that all our sufficiency comes from Christ because He is always the same, never wavering. He is always on the throne. We get to have the confidence that we are adequate all the time just because we are God's daughter and we believe in Christ (2 Corinthians 3:4–5).

I am filled with hope when I believe in what Christ died to give me. Jesus absolutely is our hope because we know that in Him, we have an abundance of blessings, joy, and peace. When we always have hope, we can keep persevering as long as we are alive (Romans 15:13).

I am confident that God will bring every good thing in my life to fullness. Jesus came to fulfill the law and prophecies from the Old Testament. He was the last and final sacrifice that had been described in the Book of Isaiah. Now you get to trust that God will bring every good work to a full completion in you until the day Christ returns (Philippians 1:6).

Confidence from Christ

I have glorious riches in Christ. Christ empowers you to be everything you were meant to be. When you tap into Him, He releases contentment and peace over your beloved heart (Philippians 4:19).

The same power lives within me that raised Christ from the dead. Realize that you can enter any room, answer any call, and rise up after any fall because the same power that raised Jesus to life, lives in you (Romans 8:11).

I have a heavenly mind-set, the mind of Christ. You have been given the mind of Christ, which means you can have direct communication with God. Expect miracles and be unfazed by rejection (1 Corinthians 2:16).

I am crowned. The Lord has crowned you with His endless love and mercy. Nothing you do can change His love for you; His mercies are new every morning. Mercy and love lead to transformation, not condemnation (Psalm 103:2–4).

I have permission to release God's love and authority when I walk in any space. You have been unified in Christ, which enables you to overcome fear with confidence, usher peace into a place of chaos, and bring the beauty of hope in realms of hopelessness (Colossians 2:10).

Confidence like Christ

I can live life unworried and undaunted. You don't have to be intimidated by people, situations, or life when your life is hidden in Christ (2 Timothy 1:7).

I believe and expect miracles to happen. When Jesus prayed for healing and increase, He didn't wonder if it would happen or pray really long prayers. He commanded it would be done in a few short words and it was (John 5: 8–9).

I remain unmoved when I could easily get offended. Almost everywhere Jesus taught, He was also mocked and ridiculed by the elite religious leaders. He never, however, got offended, reacted out of line, or allowed the offense to intimidate or fester inside him (Galatians 1:10).

I am confident enough that I am content not getting recognition because I know God sees me. Our confidence doesn't need to be found in the approval or recognition from others, Instagram likes, or how many followers we have on social media. It isn't found in honors, accolades, or invitations. As long as we are doing what is pleasing in God's sight, we can be confident that His applause is all we need (Matthew 6:4–6). In what area can you surrender acknowledgment or recognition?

I am courageous because I trust God will strengthen me. The night Jesus was praying at the Mount of Olives, He asked God if there was another way to fulfill His destiny other than suffering on the cross. When God didn't answer, Jesus moved forward. This task didn't come easily because He was fully human, too. He would feel every lashing of the whip and endure three fiery and dark days in hell. But He trusted God's plan and courageously allowed the Pharisees to arrest Him so His destiny could be fulfilled for the sake of the world (Luke 22:42–43). What is God calling you to be courageous for?

I am so confident in God's protection that I am free to bless my enemies. When Jesus was arrested, His disciple Peter cut off the ear of one of the guards in an attempt to defend Him. But even in this moment, Jesus healed the ear back on the guard. I'm sure you have experienced gossip or the betrayal of a friend. You can be so confident in God to avenge a wrong that you don't have to defend yourself to get revenge. Never even in our weakest moment of vulnerability has God forsaken us (Luke 22:51).

When we have the confidence that is in Christ, from Christ, and like Christ, we can do all things through He who strengthens us. I encourage you to meditate on these truths. When you are feeling low or insecure, turn back to these pages and read the declarations of what you have living with in you. All you have to do is believe and become aware of it.

> *When we have the confidence that is in Christ, from Christ, and like Christ, we can do all things through He who strengthens us.*

Christlike Confidence = The Sparkle Effect

Prayer

Dear Father:

Thank You for giving me the gift of Christ so that I have an unwavering source of confidence. Lord, I want to only seek my confidence and identity in You because You are my real Father—the One who created me, and the One who will bring me home. God, thank You for the perfect plan You have for me.

Please fill me up with the same trust, courage, and faith that Jesus had when He wept that night on the rock at the Mount of Olives. He trusted You so much. He had a Godly confidence because He wasn't focused on Himself; He was focused on having a relationship with me one day. Just thinking of this brings me to tears. Why are You so good to me? I love You so much.

Please help me to abandon self-centeredness so I can have the peace to bless my enemies, whether bullies, mean girls, or offenders. I want to exude Christlike confidence everywhere I go, no matter my circumstances. Thank You for answering prayers that are in alignment with Your perfect will. Amen!

Wonder Words

"This is my command—be strong and courageous! Do not be afraid or discouraged. For the Lord your God is with you wherever you go."

—Joshua 1:9

But blessed are those who trust in the Lord
and have made the Lord their hope and confidence.
They are like trees planted along a riverbank,
with roots that reach deep into the water.
Such trees are not bothered by the heat
or worried by long months of drought.
Their leaves stay green,
and they never stop producing fruit.

—Jeremiah 17:7–8

For I can do everything through Christ, who gives me strength.

—Philippians 4:13

And we are confident that he hears us whenever we ask for anything that pleases him. And since we know he hears us when we make our requests, we also know that he will give us what we ask for.

—1 John 5:14–15

chapter 13

Sparkle with God-Centeredness

God's in His heaven, all's right with the world.

— *Anne, from Anne of Green Gables*

We are incredible creations who are capable of incredible things. There are many days, and even weeks, I fall into autopilot and self-reliance because I think I am capable of producing good works on my own. Everyone, including nonbelievers, is able to create magnificent things, not because they don't need God, but because they are made in the image of the Creator. We are all *creations* by the *Creator*. We may be able to make do on our own, but if we want to be truly powerful, free, and impactful, then it is critical to plug into and to stay plugged into God.

The problem is, many of us don't even know how to seek God. I learned many years ago that God still speaks to us today just like He did to His children in the Bible. He speaks to *you*. Since I learned how to hear His voice and tap into His presence, my life has been completely changed. (More on this later in the chapter.)

One November, Kris and I took a long weekend trip up to northern California, where the temperature drop reminded us that it *was* autumn. We nestled in a cozy Airbnb with some of our closest friends and set our sights on reconnecting with our own hearts and the heart of God. We were really blessed that our friends poured into us that weekend. They prayed over us, spoke life-giving words of encouragement, and led us into a time of reflection.

I needed this weekend so much. I was running on empty, trying to do it all. I was so busy and was speeding past my morning time with God. I was staying up later at night to return texts and e-mails, so my phone was the last thing I saw when I fell asleep. I found myself paying the price for neglecting quality time with God. Just as your relationship with a loved one will suffer if you don't spend time together, your relationship and overall centeredness will falter when you aren't seeking God.

All the noise, demands, and distractions of even the good things in my life were muffling His voice. I was thirsty to hear clearly from God. I prayed for His voice to be clear before we returned from our trip. For the first few days, I felt like there was a wall between us and I was so discouraged. *Was He mad at me? Had He forgotten me? Had He turned his back on me because I turned mine on Him?* Have you ever asked those questions? When you did, what did you find out?

Finally, I realized I was allowing my fear to stand between us. I was afraid that He didn't want to speak to me anymore. But those thoughts aren't true at all. I snapped out of it. When I surrendered my fear and reminded myself that He never leaves or forsakes me, I heard Him.

I spent two hours asking God questions, listening for His answers, and going through waves of feeling love. At the end, I felt completely drained, yet totally full and satisfied. We went to church during our getaway and spent time singing praise and worship. I could feel the weight I was carrying float off me. I wish I could just live in this place that nurtures such a connection with

God all the time. But I could stay only long enough to get re-centered, recharged, and reset. God and I still had a mission to fulfill back in Los Angeles and I'd been reminded of it. The time away to focus on Him brought our relationship and my clarity of purpose to a new level. I felt ready to take on the world with my heavenly mind-set.

You were created to connect with the Creator. You were made for purpose in partnership. When you aren't connecting with Him, your well runs dry and life becomes harder. We are not made to live in survival mode or autopilot, going through the motions trying to make it to the next day only to do it all over again.

When the eyes of your heart are opened to see things the way God does, everything will fall into place.

> *When the eyes of your heart are opened to see things the way God does, everything will fall into place.*

Here are some powerful ways to connect with the Presence of God, the Holy Spirit, and Jesus.

1. Worship.

For me, singing praise and worship is the most powerful part of church. The reason is because the heart of God speaks to me when I'm singing. We have the mind of Christ, and when we worship the One who made us, we rise above ourselves and thoughts, welcome or unwelcome. Worship gets us into the presence of God because our focus is off the visible and glides into the invisible realm, which is where we can see the most clearly. Everyone we see is charged by the unseen. Sometimes in worship, I close my eyes and see images that inspire me or I sense God nudging me in an area of life that needs change.

For instance, one Sunday I asked God to speak to me in worship. As we were singing, I heard Him say in my spirit, "Consecrate yourself." I saw a vision of myself handing a glass of wine to Him. In exchange, I received His presence anew. That moment, I began fasting from wine and continued for sixty days. During that time, God gave me the idea for this book.

Encountering God in worship is biblical. Psalm 24:6 says, "Such people may seek you and worship in your presence, O God of Jacob" (NLT). But in the NLT version, the word *worship* is interchangeable with the word *face*. When we worship God, we get to encounter God's face.

Application: Pray and ask God to show up during worship; remind Him of His promise to you that says "when you seek me, you will find me when you seek me with your whole heart." Ask Him in advance for how you would like Him to speak to you. To get really clear, I will write a line in my journal of a question I have before worship begins. Then if you can, try to close your eyes in worship so you can get lost in the words. Keep your journal nearby, so you can write down what you heard, felt, or sensed.

2. Seek uninterrupted silence to listen.

If you really want to have powerful days, don't look to others or books for affirmations anymore. Go straight to the face of God because you can. God longs to speak Truth to us. Sometimes we get caught up in *talking to* Him and forget to be quiet and *listen to* Him.

Application: Before you start your day, lean back and close your eyes. Imagine yourself under a waterfall. The water streaming down is the Living water filled with God's love and healing power. Imagine it flowing through you. Soak in how He wants to minister to your heart. Then ask, "Jesus, what do You call me?" Take the first positive word. Then hold out your hands and say, "Jesus, what do You have for me?" You will probably understand the significance right away, but if you don't, ask Him, "What does this mean?" Always journal what you hear.

3. Read the Bible.

The Word is never boring. It is full of fresh and exciting adventures for your mind and heart. If it is hard for you to connect when reading or difficult to understand, ask God to give you the spiritual eyes and wisdom to understand it. When you read, ask God what it means to you and how it applies to your life. I really love enhancing my morning time under the waterfall with Scripture. You can do this, too.

Application: Ask the Holy Spirit to reveal a verse that God wants to speak to you, wait to see a Scripture, like "Psalm 123:4," pop into your head, then turn to it. Another fun way I read the Word is the first thing I do when I wake up in the morning is ask Holy Spirit to give me a page number. Then I turn to that page in the Bible and read it. Almost always, there is something that is exactly what I need.

4. Praise and give thanks.

It's easy to get down on ourselves and feel discouraged when we aren't where we want to be. We can lose hope and say, "I might as well just give up." That is precisely how the enemy will feed on our discouragement. That's why focusing on what God has done for and through us is so refreshing. We are able to look back at our old selves, where we first started on the journey, and think, "Wow, I have come so far. I'm not where I want to be, but I've come a long way."

Application: Make a list of all the gifts He has given you. Also, make a list of all the ways He has grown you and healed you.

There is nothing more sparkle-infusing than spending time with God and basking in His love. When we take the time to center our minds and hearts on God, we will continue to be transformed more and more into the image of Christ.

Centering Your Heart within God's = The Sparkle Effect

Prayer

Dear Father:

I pray that You would speak to me so clearly in the way You created me to hear You. Please help me to create margin in my life so I have the time to silence everything around me and tune into Your voice. I know that I can't fully carry out the mission You have assigned me if I'm not in sync with You. Father, I long for my heart to beat as one with Yours. I want nothing more. I just ask that You would be faithful to Your promises that say You will show up and make Your presence known when I wholeheartedly seek You. I declare I am infused with the Holy Spirit that ignites wisdom and discernment as my guide. Amen.

Wonder Words

As the secrets of their hearts are laid bare. So they will fall down and worship God, exclaiming, "God is really among you!"

—1 Corinthians 14:25

God is spirit, and his worshipers must worship in the Spirit and in truth.

—John 4:24

There will no longer be any curse; and the throne of God and of the Lamb will be in it, and His bond-servants will serve Him; they will see His face, and His name will be on their foreheads.

—Revelation 22:3–5

chapter 14

Sparkle with Focus

Comparison is the thief of all joy.
—*Eleanor Roosevelt*

Eleanor Roosevelt's statement "Comparison is the thief of all joy" couldn't be truer. We know we're not supposed to compare ourselves, but sometimes we feel powerless to the urge.

Comparison crept into my joyful young self when I entered middle school. Adolescence is when we start caring about what boys think and say about us; we want to be the girl they like but it's also a good idea not to incite jealousy among the girls in the process.

I remember looking around at the girls who seemed to be confident and have it all together. I know, who has it all together as a thirteen-year-old? I thought they did, though. I compared my clothes, the way I talked, the way I acted, and things I liked to them.

Comparison will drive us crazy and make us sick because it's a constant taunting that we aren't measuring up to the *cool kids*.

I remember my mama saying to me, "Quit trying to be like _____." I would get so mad that (1) she didn't think I was naturally cool on my own, and (2) that she could so easily call my bluff.

Comparison doesn't stop in middle school. It can stay with us well into adult life, crippling the little girl heart inside us that longs to thrive and dream. When we try to be like other people or operate in their strengths and gifting, we aren't being true to ourselves, and those around us can easily sense something is off because we aren't being authentic.

I believe we compare ourselves to others to see if we're doing okay. We feel good if we are better and terrible if we aren't. Comparison is judging others and ourselves. It steals our ability to discover who we really are, enjoy who we are, and own who we are.

When I moved to Los Angeles, I set my sights on TV hosting and making it in the entertainment industry. I felt like I needed to prove myself to who knows who. Maybe there was a tinge of "I'll show you" in response to the people who criticized me on message boards during my year as Miss USA. But I had something to prove to myself, too. Do you ever feel that way?

I took hosting classes from the most respected studio in the industry, secured top agents, and made a hosting reel and a résumé. I was going out on auditions, but not booking. I remember scrolling through my Twitter to check certain updates to see what others were booking. Still, I was booking print and commercial work consistently, which was a huge blessing. I was able to pay all my bills, live by myself, and still have income left over to put into savings. But I wasn't able to clearly see what a blessing it was then or experience the joy of it, because I was too busy comparing myself to someone I wanted to be like. It's interesting—I've experienced that when I don't give God praise and honor for what He's giving me, He often allows it to be taken away until I get a heart check.

I am highly critical of myself, which also leads to a tendency to be critical of others. Comparison breeds a spirit of criticism, which can lead to subtle or full-blown arrogance when we're rockin' it or self-pity when we aren't measuring up. The game of comparison is such a roller coaster.

In the months of preparation leading up to Miss USA, I knew I would have a major problem keeping a winning mind-set if I didn't get this comparison issue on lockdown.

Can you imagine spending three weeks with fifty other women, all beautiful, and not comparing yourself? How in the world does a young woman handle the pressures of everyday life, much less a concentrated scenario of direct competition?

You don't have to let comparison steal your sparkle. Here is how you can defeat it:

1. Compete with yourself.

At a week-long mental management seminar, I learned this valuable truth that was a total game changer for me. No matter the scenario, life isn't a competition with others; it's a competition with yourself. There is no way we can use other people as the mirror to see ourselves. Everything you do is about being the best version of yourself. You have to look in the mirror right in front of you. Look at how intricate and wonderful you are. Ask yourself what you would be like if you were living to your fullest potential. Imagine her. Then get laser focused, and use the imagination of your best self as your inspiration. I've learned to stop looking around me to see how I compare with others, and instead to look upward at Jesus and to the woman He meant for me to become.

2. Realize that you can't control outside factors.

Comparison is a waste of time. Other people are external factors that are outside of our control. We can't control the girls who intimidate us. We also can't control the voices of criticism we may encounter in life. We can't control the onlookers who use their spare time to size us up and rank us next to someone else. The girl who seems to keep stealing your limelight isn't going to get any less attractive as you become more bitter. But you will.

One year at Miss USA, there was a titleholder everyone was talking about. She was beautiful, confident, successful, and had a lot of hype. She ended up winning. A few years later, I talked to some of the girls who competed with her. They said they talked about her amongst themselves through the competition, which took them out of a winning, focused mind-set. One girl said it best, "We gave her all the power."

Don't give your power away! You can't control people, but you can control your actions and your response. Stop wasting your time wishing that girl would stop shining so bright. Her light doesn't blow yours out unless you let it, so you better keep sparkling! There is plenty of room for more light.

I know it's hard to stop yourself from wanting to control things or people—believe me, I've been there. Sometimes, I still have to catch myself and re-focus on *my* lane.

Maybe you don't know what your lane is so you look to others for inspiration. Now is a good time to ask God to show you. But even while you are waiting for clear guidance on a certain path, one thing is for sure. Your lane is to love God, love others, and love yourself. When feelings of inspiration begin to turn into feelings of enervation, that's when you've crossed over into comparison.

Comparison doesn't help you at all, it only stirs up insecurity, anger, and regret. It ultimately disconnects you from the radiance of your true identity.

3. Focus on what you can control.

Self-control is a fruit of the Spirit. That's because we are made to manage ourselves with Godly wisdom rather than letting our feelings take the wheel. You are responsible for your thoughts, feelings, and actions. Are you being kind and uplifting to yourself? Are you focusing on who you are and how God made you? Make a list of your awesome qualities and focus on them the minute your eyes start to wander over to someone else's lane.

When you begin to compare, your sparkle dims and you actually give your power away. Don't you dare waver in the magnificent, unique woman you are! There may be someone else like you, but she isn't you. No one does you better than you.

The moment you notice you are focusing on an external factor that you can't control, like a heel breaking or a change in the program, snap your focus on how you can *handle* it. For instance, I remember preparing for an interview that was supposed to be a round-robin style, one-on-one setup. I visualized and practiced this for months. Then, when I arrived everything changed. Now, the interview was going to be with two separate panels. I wouldn't be sitting anymore, I would be standing in front of them. My natural reaction is alarm bells going off in my head. But, the Godly way is usually the opposite of what your natural reaction might be. This was a situation I couldn't control; instead, I surrendered the situation to God, pumped myself up with Queen Declarations, and *handled* it. When you can't control it, handle it.

4. Know your assets.

Realize what makes you unique. What are your best features? What makes you come alive and feel confident? We need to stop trying to be the second-rate version of someone else and be the best version of ourselves.

I remember in the sixth grade, some of the girls were talking about their new favorite song by Britney Spears. I said, "Who's Britney Spears?" They scoffed, "You don't know who Britney Spears is? You guys, did you hear that? Kristen doesn't know who Britney Spears is. What a loser!"

I remember feeling embarrassed. I tried to laugh it off, but I felt my face turning red and my whole body getting hot. My parents didn't let us listen to pop music. We were still listening to Sandi Patty, Point of Grace, and children's choir music. If you don't know who these artists are, it's okay—you were probably a cool kid.

A seemingly trivial moment for others was a defining moment for me that caused me to question who I was and ultimately to hide who I was. From that point forward, I lived in the tension of feeling set apart by God and set apart negatively. I wanted to blend in enough to make it through the school day with people to talk to, and friends to sit with at lunch. So I decided to learn how to be cool by picking up on mannerisms of the cool kids. I have a little actress in me, you do, too. I became a pro at faking it 'til I made it. Have you? Faking it is draining, as you may know. You don't have to fake it though! Why would you do that? You're too good in your true design. You might just need to dig in to find the magic in who you are.

> *We will never become our best selves if we are focused on trying to be liked.*

We will never become our best selves if we are focused on trying to be liked. If this resonates with you, I wish I could reach through the pages and pull the effervescent essence of you out through the layers of who you thought you needed to be. But this is a task you must tackle. It's time to rediscover who God designed you to be. This journey begins when you schedule time alone with yourself and ask some real questions. Here are some to get you started:

- What are things I say or do that make me feel like an imposter?
- Why are these lies?
- When is the first time I felt I needed to do this?
- What part(s) of me do I feel I need to hide?
- What will happen if people knew I really didn't like certain things?
- What will happen if I start saying NO in circumstances where I've usually said YES?
- Even if the worst scenario comes true, can I trust God to come through?

5. Want others to be their best, too.

In our quest to win, succeed, and be loved, we mistakenly think that means other people have to fail. We can even find ourselves hoping and wishing for others' demise. I remember that when I started my blog, *She Is More*, I was so excited. One night, I was lying in bed and I asked the Lord what He wanted to call my future ministry. Kris told me I needed to make my then blog at kristenjdalton.com bigger than myself. As I started to dose, I heard a faint whisper in my spirit...*She is more precious than rubies...She is more.* I jolted awake. That was it! *She is More.* God had just spoken it to me because I surely am not clever enough to come up with that on my own. I had one of my first God ideas and it was exhilarating. I felt so special the Lord was personally guiding me. I was full steam ahead on getting it started. I had my site redesigned, published three articles a week, and even organized a team of writers that began to contribute weekly. A couple months into it, I noticed other blogs popping up that were using similar wording, and some that were downright copying. Let's just say God had to deal with me on this. I couldn't write on confidence and character while letting my feathers get ruffled by people who appeared to be walking in *my* calling.

The thing I learned is, it isn't about *my* calling or *my* purpose or *my* anything. All of everything belongs to God and He simply asks us to steward a need using the talents He's given us. He doesn't just ask one person. He asks a lot of people. He pretty much asks whoever will say yes. Wanting others to fail for the goal of winning is denying the very God who inspires us to do anything good.

When you get the mind-set shift that what you do is about expanding God's Kingdom, no matter who else is doing it and how they're doing it, you will begin experiencing joy in seeing others succeed. There is freedom in wanting to see the best in others instead of being intimidated by them. When your heart is pure in your motives, the sparkle will shine through your eyes.

6. Filter your social media.

It is wise to guard your heart and mind against things that trigger feelings of insecurity or comparison. With instant and addicting access to open our social media apps and scroll through others' photos, we are more susceptible than ever to comparing ourselves.

If there are certain people who evoke negative feelings in you, go ahead and unfollow or mute those accounts. Sometimes we have to take proactive, precautionary measures to stay on track with what God is calling us to do. We don't need to feel guilty or apologize for it either. There is wisdom in creating the space you need to keep a pure heart.

Don't let the devil take you into a downward spiral through comparison. It's a silent trap and you deserve more than to tear yourself apart.

As Galatians 6:4–5 reminds us, "Each of you must examine your own actions. Then you can be proud of your own accomplishments without comparing yourself to others. Assume your own responsibility."

Focusing on Becoming Your Best = The Sparkle Effect

Prayer

Dear Father:

I praise You because I am uniquely and wonderfully made. Lord, help me to not fall into the sin of comparing myself to others that leads to envy. I realize that I am the only one able to respond to the call on my life and to being the best version of myself. I don't want to stay miserable in feeling sorry for myself. Self-pity can be addicting and I like the attention it gets me, but I know I will eventually be left behind if I don't rise up and take ownership of my life. I want to honor You by honoring myself by keeping my mind focused on You. Change my heart to genuinely want the best for others because I can see Your glory in their lives, too. Help me to surrender my pride, criticism, and judgment so I can just be open to what You want to do in life. God, I don't mind if I get praise or accolades in this life, but I really just want to live for Your applause. Thank You for helping me focus on You to see what the best version of myself looks like. Amen.

Wonder Words

You shall not covet your neighbor's house; you shall not covet your neighbor's wife, or his male servant, or his female servant, or his ox, or his donkey, or anything that is your neighbor's.

—Exodus 20:17

Not that we dare to classify or compare ourselves with some of those who are commending themselves. But when they measure themselves by one another and compare themselves with one another, they are without understanding.

—2 Corinthians 10:12

Do nothing from rivalry or conceit, but in humility count others more significant than yourselves.

—Philippians 2:3

chapter 15

Sparkle with Security

It takes courage to be who you truly are.

—*Merida, from Brave*

Envy is one of the most ensnaring, debilitating sins to live in. It is easy to fall into envy without realizing it, but it is so very poisonous once it's taken root. It can make us sick, unproductive, and unattractive—which is probably where the expression "green with envy" originates.

Jealousy can cause a lot of different emotions and behaviors, such as anger, resentment, gossip, and self-hate. With unprecedented exposure to the good part of other people's lives on social media, it may seem almost impossible not to be tempted into jealousy every day. But the Bible calls envy a deadly sin for a reason. James 3:14–16 says: "But if you are bitterly jealous and there is selfish ambition in your heart, don't cover up the truth with boasting and lying. For jealousy and selfishness are not God's kind of wisdom. Such things are earthly, unspiritual, and demonic. For wherever there is jealousy and selfish ambition, there you will find disorder and evil of every kind" (NLT).

This Scripture reinforces that jealousy isn't a petty, silly girl is-sue to be easily dismissed. It says that jealousy is *demonic* and that evil always comes from it. If we are to sparkle with security, we must guard ourselves against jealousy.

Yet no matter how successful, everyone is susceptible to envy. I thought if I published a book, I would feel complete in success. I could relax for the rest of my life and pop out babies. Nope, that definitely wasn't the case. Because then, I needed to write a follow-up guide to go with it. When that was done, I needed to do something else. What is it for you?

Creating new products and chasing new dreams aren't wrong in and of themselves. It's our motives that matter. Do we have something to prove? Is our jealousy of that other girl's success motivating our goals? If we aren't rooted in who and *whose* we are, our quest to "one up" the girl next to you will be a never-ending roller coaster.

Jealousy can be a vicious cycle. Once you get whatever it is you think will make you proud or content, that satisfaction will be short lived if that is your main source of fulfillment. Get-ting what we want isn't the remedy to cure jealousy. Like a painkiller—it only masks the symptoms momentarily. The real healing happens in the depths of our heart. You can pretend like you are confident and content by donning a smile and congratu-lating your friends on their blessings, but if your heart is jealous, then you are dying on the inside. God doesn't care how good we are at pretending. He sees the inner thoughts of our heart, and that is where your freedom and joy begin...or end. There is noth-ing more liberating and beautifying than breaking free of envy.

I have struggled a lot with this issue. My husband would sometimes come home and start talking about the successes of others, even my friends. Oftentimes, I'd stop him mid-sentence and ask that he please not share that news with me. I didn't want to hear about it because it made me feel insufficient, and that led to my feeling and acting inferior when I was around them in person. Do you ever find yourself feeling or acting awkward around someone you have private jealousy toward?

That is absolutely no way to live; I hated being like that. We don't have to be like that! I wanted to genuinely feel happy for them in my heart and not let their achievements cause me to question my value. So why didn't I? What was holding me back?

Jealousy is an open door for the enemy to sow seeds of evil. You can probably even feel it coming over you when you let jealousy in the door. I wanted to keep that door shut when jealousy came knocking so I set out to learn how. The truths I discovered have worked. I won't say I never struggle with it now, but it is certainly much rarer. They can work for you, too!

Here are five ways to break free from envy and gain security so you can continue stepping into the radiance of your true identity:

1. Trust God.

Truly and wholeheartedly trusting God is the strongest key to lock jealousy from your life. We may think God loves someone else more than He loves us when it seems they walk with a cloud of favor around them. But that is an illusion the enemy wants you to buy into. Focus on the ways you've been able to trust Him in your life. The King has assigned each of us our portion and given us grace for each gift we have.

We are not all meant to have a million followers on Instagram, marry a rich athlete, or be a movie star. Some people have a grace on their life to handle more attention or notoriety in their respective field, and it isn't up to us to decide if they are deserving of it or not. As the psalmist tells us, "LORD, you alone are my portion and my cup; you make my lot secure. The boundary lines have fallen for me in pleasant places; surely I have a delightful inheritance" (Psalm 16:5–6 NIV).

God is good and He has good reasons for the lot He has assigned you. Decide to trust that He has your best interest at heart.

2. Take ownership of your life.

Envy can prompt us to ask, "That is something I really want; why don't I have it?" Envy can reveal regret we haven't taken action on something we want. When we see someone else produce an idea that we had or go on a vacation we have been dreaming of, our feeling of envy could be the result of being mad at ourselves for not taking action. Instead of doing something about it, we spend our time criticizing them and blaming God.

Being inactive in the dreams God has put on your heart doesn't allow God to breathe on your activity. Once I started doing what God was telling me to do, I gave Him the chance to bless my work and show me His favor. Even if the conditions aren't perfect yet, take action and ownership of your life so God can show you His blessings. It's never too late.

3. Have the right idea of what success is.

Everyone has a story, a calling, and a way of getting there. Success is showing up every day and doing the best you can. Success is consistently operating within your anointing and trusting the results to God. Even though society measures success through outcomes and numbers, that isn't how it's measured in the heavenly realms, which is where it matters. Success in the Kingdom is measured by the condition of our hearts and whether we put our faith to work.

4. Her success is not your failure.

It is a cutthroat world we live in. Sports teams compete; we compete for college acceptance, for a pageant title, for a promotion, for that scholarship, for that guy, for the "best friend" status. How in the world are we not supposed to feel like a failure when someone else wins, especially at something you really want? In all my years of competing and being rejected, I *had* to learn that others' success isn't my failure. Otherwise I'd go crazy! And it's true. Will you just look up the biography of a person you admire the most? See how many times he or she experienced a loss. The way you handle loss determines how you win.

Considering someone else's success to be our failure is an indication that our motive has been mangled. The Bible cautions against selfish ambition, and emphasizes the power of a pure heart. Get excited when other people succeed because they are a testimony to how good God is to all of us in His perfect timing. If God is good to them, He'll be good to you.

5. Be grateful.

I believe when we take time to notice all the ways God blesses us, there won't be any space left to be jealous. I am a competitive, results-driven visionary, so I constantly set new goals and want to do more in a bigger, and better way. Dreaming big is great; but it's important to do it with a queen's mind-set. A queen doesn't dream big because she isn't rich enough, pretty enough, or good enough. She dreams from a place of thankfulness for the position she is in to impact others. It keeps the sparkle in your eyes to dream from a place of thankfulness as opposed to lack. God is the biggest dreamer and wants to co-create with you.

A secure heart allows you to operate out of peace and purity. It is beneficial to be thankful not only for your blessings, but also for the blessings other people are experiencing.

Every morning, I make a list of all the gifts and blessings in my life. From my hot coffee, to my husband who poured it, to the bed I'm journaling in. A great book on this is *A Thousand Gifts* by Ann Voskamp. Make it your practice every day to write down all your gifts and focus on what God is giving, instead of what you're lacking.

> *Make it your practice every day to write down all your gifts and focus on what God is giving, instead of what you're lacking.*

Get excited for what God is doing in the lives of others as well because that puts your focus on how awesome He is. You are a daughter of God, and the enemy will use jealousy to poison you, so don't feed it with your thoughts. Take captive every thought that isn't of God and turn it into a loving, positive, power thought.

You can do this. Jealousy isn't serving you, and God will answer your prayer and pursuit to deliver you from it. Security is the opposite of jealousy, and it is your royal inheritance.

Take Action: Make a list of the people you are jealous of. Then begin to pray for them. Ask God to help you trust Him. Notice how your heart begins to soften and become more secure, ultimately releasing your sparkle.

Security = The Sparkle Effect

Prayer

Dear Father:

You know my heart so well. I can't hide from You that I deal with feelings of jealousy and inadequacy. Sometimes, I feel like You have overlooked me and continue to bless the same people with more all the time. When is it my turn? When do I get my break? But You are sovereign and true. Please forgive me for being mad at You. I know You love me. I trust You and I will choose to trust You even when I am in a season of lack. God, please help me not to look at my friends and covet what they have. Please open up a well of newfound gratitude within me; You have blessed me so abundantly. Father, help me to discern where I need to take action and where I need to surrender. I want to be content and be genuinely happy for others. Thank You for the work You are doing in me right now in Jesus' name, Amen.

Wonder Words

A peaceful heart leads to a healthy body; jealousy is like cancer in the bones.   —Proverbs 14:30

Anger is cruel, and wrath is like a flood, but jealousy is even more dangerous.

—Proverbs 27:4

Then I observed that most people are motivated to success because they envy their neighbors. But this, too, is meaningless—like chasing the wind.

—Ecclesiastes 4:4

You are jealous of one another and quarrel with each other. Doesn't that prove you are controlled by your sinful nature? Aren't you living like people of the world?

—1 Corinthians 3:3

Pay careful attention to your own work, for then you will get the satisfaction of a job well done, and you won't need to compare yourself to anyone else. For we are each responsible for our own conduct.

—Galatians 6:4

chapter 16

Sparkle with Thankfulness

Look at that sea, girls—all silver and shadow
and vision of things not seen. We couldn't
enjoy its loveliness any more if we had millions
of dollars and ropes of diamonds.

— *Anne, from Anne of Green Gables*

One of the most unbecoming qualities is entitlement. I
attended a Millennial marketing conference and listened to companies present their data on Millennial consumer behavior and
trends. There were many qualities used to describe us, but "entitled" was the prevalent theme.

The Millennial generation's attitude of entitlement means we
expect things to be given to us and done for us without doing
much to earn it. While we absolutely should have a standard in
the way we are treated and should expect appropriate compensa-
tion for our work, a sincere attitude of gratitude is the real game
changer to a life full of blessing.

Getting what we want without working for it definitely results
in entitlement and thanklessness. It's like the obnoxious young
girl, Veruca Salt, in the movie *Charlie and the Chocolate Factory*.
Her father is wealthy and overindulges her every whim. She

doesn't have an ounce of sparkle to her because she has become spoiled and expectant.

There are other reasons that lead to thanklessness, too. When we have been wronged in life, we can become cold and emotionless. We employ different tactics to get back at the world or to protect ourselves. Working to achieve success and status is one way we try to do that. When we finally get it, we don't bask in the goodness of God as we should. Instead, our eyes fixate on the next rung to climb.

There may be certain people in our lives who trigger feelings of inadequacy or unfairness. For instance, when I competed in pageants, I seemed to lose to brunettes. Afterward, I was told things like, "You come off as fake. We're not sure if we believe your résumé. Maybe consider dying your hair."

I remember feeling like I needed to downplay my bubbly personality in order to be taken seriously. I had this fire in me to prove that I was smart and relatable, without dying my hair. It was a consuming struggle and I learned that God had bigger things for me to do with my energy.

Is there a lie that has been spoken over you that fuels your ambition? Is there a certain kind of people you want to prove yourself to? Do you imagine their reaction when you prove them wrong? Try to remember that it is not your calling to fight against the lies of others. While you can use them as healthy motivation, don't let it be your sole motivation. Instead, focus on the gifts God has given you and cultivate them for His purpose. Shift your focus upward and rejoice in His blessings.

Losing trust in people has a huge impact on us. As a young girl, I was trusting by nature. I loved people and believed the best about them. Even after being mistreated or rejected, I'd still get excited to see them. I'm not exactly sure when it happened or what the tipping point was, but one day the hurt-but-trusting girl in me turned into a suspicious, self-sufficient "lone wolf." When we don't trust people, we don't let them help us.

Have you ever felt like most people want to help you only to get something from you? After I won Miss North Carolina USA, it was amazing how many people wanted to be on my team to help me prepare for the Miss USA competition. I thought, *Where were you before?*

In one sense, having boundaries and discernment is a good thing. It's important to be selective about who we bring close to us. It has been a lesson I've learned the hard way at times. For instance, I've been shocked and completely let down by people I thought I could trust. Not just people, but those I thought had my best interest at heart.

(In the following story, I'm going to keep the details vague because in any experience, our feelings and the way we process them are what matter.)

In one season of my life, I had the chance to finally work with a group of people I'd always admired to prepare for a certain goal. I was thrilled. One weekend, we had a brainstorming session and I couldn't wait to hear their insight for me. But the rug was quickly ripped from underneath my feet when the group of people I admired called me into a meeting. I brought my notebook and pen and was ready to take notes! When I sat down, I quickly sensed a daunting energy in the room and realized this meeting wasn't what I had hoped for. My mentors began to accuse and expose me in front of others. I felt like I was eight years old again. I remember feeling shocked and wide-eyed as they all came at me, turning on me. When I tried defending myself, they refused to believe me. I was absolutely heartbroken. Why would they say these things? Why were they attacking me? These were individuals I had always looked up to, whom I had opened up to, and whom I was excited to work with. I wanted to be on their team. I remember going to a bathroom and crying very hard after that.

I booked an earlier flight home. From that day on, I shut down on people who wanted to help me and made up my mind that I was on my own. This was a mistake because it made it harder for me to accept help. When we don't accept help, we become more self-reliant and thus can become less thankful.

Have you ever talked to someone who reached a level of success and heard them say something along the lines, "Thank you, I did it all on my own!" Maybe they do truly feel that way—for a time I felt I was on my own—but no one ever gets anywhere completely by themselves. Thankfully, I had my family and some special friends. I hope there is someone near who is there for you, too, and with whom you can express gratitude for their help in all you accomplish.

But if you're reeling from hurt that prevents you from living with a thankful heart, I understand the desire to be vindicated for that injustice. I also know that even if you get the redemption or even revenge you seek, you will not be satisfied. When someone betrays our trust, it can cause us to deny connection with truly good-hearted people. If you get to your destination without appreciating all the sweet moments and generous people who made up your journey, you've walked right into a trap the enemy carefully laid out for you. We fall into this trap when we are too focused on proving something to those who are completely oblivious to the real estate they've taken in our mind.

Think about Maleficent, the evil queen in Disney's *Snow White.* She spends years and years making sure she stays the most beautiful woman in the land. She lacks gratitude and is selfish. She spends all her free time plotting how she will kill her stepdaughter, who becomes a threat to her as she grows in beauty. While she is brewing poisonous concoctions, poison is consuming her heart. In her quest to kill Snow White, her sparkle dies instead. All the time she spent contriving was such a waste and led to her demise. Imagine if she had spent time mentoring Snow

White and grooming her to become the next queen. What a legacy she could have left instead. Her time would have been spent meaningfully and productively. She would have been sparkling with goodness and generosity, which could only illuminate, not detract from, her physical beauty.

I've worked with girls to help them address their lack of appreciation. I've been told by them, "I really am thankful; I just don't know how to express it." There may be a wall up that you've subconsciously built to protect yourself. Maybe you don't want someone to think you need them, because needing help makes you vulnerable to betrayal or hurt. Or, maybe you don't think you are worthy of help or kindness, so you deflect it. Whatever your wall is made of, it prevents you from receiving kindness, making genuine connection with others, and expressing gratitude. Maybe it's pride, or maybe it's a defense from all the years you were hurt. But you have to find a way to be grateful. Feeling and expressing thankfulness is imperative to having sparkle in your eyes. Thankfulness starts in your heart and then flows out.

> *Feeling thankful and expressing it are imperative to having sparkle in your eyes.*

Here is how:

1. Take your focus off the competition.

Release the need to win for the sake of beating your competitors. For example, when I go to auditions, it's like the scene from

LaLa Land where Emma Stone's character shows up to the casting and all the girls in the waiting room have the same look, hair color, and attire. It feels like there is no way to win. It can feel like that so much sometimes in life. That's why we can't get distracted by the competition and instead just be thankful for the opportunity. Being thankful in the midst of high stakes keeps us present and connected.

2. Focus on people.

You were designed to make the world a better place through your story, your gifts, and your heart. Notice the tiniest thing someone does for you to make your life better. Think about how your life would be different if they weren't there. Acknowledge the time, energy, and resources that are expended by the people who do things for you in sweet and thoughtful ways.

3. Ask if you would do what they are doing.

Now put yourself in their shoes. Imagine yourself doing exactly what they do or have done for you. We can take family members for granted so easily because we think, *Well, it's my mom, she should do my laundry.* But family is where our character is refined and revealed the most. Your family members are doing the best with what they have and deserve to be appreciated. Recognize that no one owes you anything, and someone you take for granted could be gone in an instant.

4. Start doing for others.

We don't realize how much someone is doing for us until we do and serve others in a similar capacity. For example, we may not know how much work goes into event planning if we have never planned something for someone else. In our head, we may think, *Well, she is a bridesmaid, that's what she is supposed to do.* Just because someone is "supposed" to do something because they volunteered or agreed doesn't mean you shouldn't be extremely thankful. If you want to have a sincere heart when appreciating others, start doing a little bit of what they are doing for someone else. Spend time with them so you can see all the details they are putting into making your life better. This is when my thankfulness was deepened to a new level for all the people who have given their time and gifts for me, especially my mother.

You absolutely are an amazing person, but it is important to remember that no one owes you anything. The Bible tells us to serve one another, but it also says to give thanks in everything. It isn't up to us to determine what anyone "should" do. Your expectation may be justified, but maintaining your heartfelt posture of thankfulness only helps you keep your peace. It also makes it more enjoyable for others to help you.

5. Let down your pride.

Pride is when we don't want anyone to know we need something. Pride is when we refuse to acknowledge someone for what they did for us or an idea they inspired. Pride is the need to be perceived like we have it all together. Pride is even selective memory and creating our own stories that satisfy our narrative that says, "I did it all on my own, I don't need you." I have absolutely struggled with this. When friends offer to help, I don't let them. The reason is because if I let them in, then they will see my mess. They will see what a mess I am. It's scary to let friends into your mess when you assume they might judge you for not having it all together. But, maybe it's because you are judging yourself too hard. Start being kind and gentle with yourself. Then letting people in won't be so scary. Even if someone does judge you, who really cares anyway? The Word says, "If God is for us, who can be against us?" (Romans 8:31 ESV).

The Lord has humbled me in huge ways, leaving me no choice but to let people into my mess. I tried planning a women's conference all by myself and almost had a nervous breakdown. I realized if I wanted it to be a success, I had to reach out to people and say those cringing words, "I need your help." I have found so much freedom and liberation in letting people see I don't have it all together all the time. There is so much joy in it! Your mess isn't that bad and it's never too messy for God. Lean on the body of Christ.

Maintaining image is exhausting and always comes before our destruction. Pride results in people leaving us because they feel undervalued or not needed. We are made for connection and interdependence (Galatians 6:2). It is a beautiful thing to let go and rejoice over the people who want to be there for you.

6. See the gifts.

It is astonishing how drastically our minds and moods can change when we shift our thoughts to our blessings in the midst of trial. When we focus on the things we are thankful for, we are agreeing with God, seeing God, and inviting God to intervene on our behalf. We have the ability to be content no matter what our circumstances are. Rather than setting a certain expectation, see every good thing that comes in as a sweet gift and cherish even the smallest generosity.

7. Remember what God has done.

Expecting God's blessings versus feeling entitled to them are two different things. Being entitled to an answered prayer can set you up for bigger disappointment. He is a good Father who gives good gifts to His children, but He also gives us what we need when we need it. That means He will answer us differently than we hope sometimes. I can tend to get over a blessing God gives me too quickly and move on to asking for the next one. He will let me book a huge commercial and instead of relishing in it and praising Him every day, I set my sights on the next prayer request. When we get so used to His goodness, we take it for granted and want more. Staying thankful for what He has already said yes to will keep us trusting of the answers to come.

When we begin to treat people like the gifts they are, relationships will strengthen and deepen. Our joy level shoots through the roof; we realize every good thing and person in our life is a gift. When we change our expectation into appreciation, our world changes.

Thankfulness = The Sparkle Effect

Prayer

Dear Father:

Tear down the walls around my heart that prevent me from feeling thankful. God, I want to see beautiful, kind, well-intentioned people as treasures and every good thing as a gift from heaven (James

1:17). *Help me to realize that I don't have to do everything on my own and that I don't have anything to prove. God, You have already won, and You make me more than a conqueror through Jesus. I pray that I can release all the hurt from my past so I can begin to let people into my heart again. I pray for the wisdom to let good in and for the humility to feel gratitude.*

I confess that I cannot do this life alone and I need people, relationships, and grace to raise me up when I am weak. Father, I pray that You will shower me with a wave of gratitude for what Jesus did on the cross for me because I most importantly want to feel thankful for You. Lord, You gently knock and wait for me to open the door to my heart—but now I am inviting You to invade it. Make me soft and humble so I can replace my expectations with appreciation. In Jesus' name, Amen.

Wonder Words

And let the peace of Christ rule in your hearts, to which indeed you were called in one body. And be thankful. Let the word of Christ dwell in you richly, teaching and admonishing one another in all wisdom, singing psalms and hymns and spiritual songs, with thankfulness in your hearts to God. And whatever you do, in word or deed, do everything in the name of the Lord Jesus, giving thanks to God the Father through him.

—Colossians 3:15–17

We always thank God for all of you and continually mention you in our prayers. We remember before our God and Father your work produced by faith, your labor prompted by love, and your endurance inspired by hope in our Lord Jesus Christ.

—1 Thessalonians 1:2–3

Give thanks in all circumstances; for this is God's will for you in Christ Jesus. Do not quench the Spirit.

—1 Thessalonians 5:18–19

Every good and perfect gift is from above, coming down from the Father of the heavenly lights, who does not change like shifting shadows.

—James 1:17

chapter 17

Sparkle with Humility

There's a belief that you're supposed to be poor,
and suffering, and show your humility. I just
don't see the Bible that way. I see that God
came and Jesus died so that we might live an
abundant life and be a blessing to others.

—*Joel Osteen*

Humility is beautiful. Humility is the trait in a lovely woman who can captivate, disarm, and love. Humility allows the God-colors to radiate from within and through your eyes.

But we often believe wrong things about what humility is. Many Christians subscribe to the idea that we aren't supposed to love ourselves, or—Heaven forbid—actually like ourselves. It's interesting how Christians will use certain Scriptures as a good reason to hide themselves or support a false belief because it's comfortable.

People who have been hurt and mistreated since they were children often continue in a cycle that repeats hurt and mistreatment because it is familiar. The moment they read Philippians 2:3, "Consider others better than yourselves," they think, *Yes; that's right, that's good, that's familiar. Others have always been better than me; I'm just lucky to serve.* But there is more to the context of that verse that is often missed.

Sometimes hurt people instill in young girls that it's bad to love or like themselves. This belief is detrimental to women and to our connection with other women. I remember watching *Anne of Green Gables* as a young girl. I loved Anne "with an e" so much. She was a spunky, bright orphan girl who was finally adopted by a foster parent when she was thirteen years old. However, when Marilla Cuthbert met her upon her arrival at the farmhouse, she was deeply disappointed to see that a girl had shown up instead of a boy.

Anne had longed to be accepted and to belong to someone her whole life. She dreamed of being in a family. Marilla reluctantly let her stay. I remember a scene in which Anne tried on a new dress Marilla had made her. Looking in the mirror, Anne exclaimed, "I look beautiful!" Marilla instantly scolded her for it. She was taught not to "say or think such things" about herself.

My heart beat faster every time Anne's spirit and spunk were squelched by someone who should have been helping her understand her true identity. It makes me wonder how girls got by in those times where their originality and understanding of self were practically forbidden. How confusing it must have been for them to be defined by a list of manners or a marital status rather than how God saw and created them. The tension was surely tormenting.

A perfect modern-day example is *Mean Girls*. The character Regina compliments Lindsay Lohan's character, Cady, and says, "And you're, like, really pretty." Cady replies, "Thank you," to which Regina returns, "So you agree? You think you're really pretty?" Caught off guard, Cady backtracks, "Oh, I don't know," because Regina is implying it's bad to think good things about yourself. Have you ever experienced something like this?

Yet on the flip side, today we hear so much about the importance of self-love. And self-love *is* important because we are loved by God. If we aren't loving and kind to ourselves, we won't be able to give love to others. The more we focus on ourselves, however, the more self-centered we become, and this only leads to idolizing ourselves above God.

Becoming too wrapped up in self-anything, even self-deprecation, is when we become susceptible to one of the deadliest sins... pride. Pride does not always express itself as arrogance. It also looks like false humility. Pride expresses itself in a variety of ways, and every one of them always leads to destruction if not caught in time (Proverbs 16:18). Destruction of our reputation, character, career, relationships, and, most importantly, our inner peace and joy.

I have often wondered how one can be confident and still remain humble. It's that quiet confidence in a woman that is so captivating and so rare. How does she do it? How is she strong and secure yet gentle and humble? The Bible calls us to be both. So how do we intertwine the two seemingly opposing qualities?

Jesus is the best example to see how this divinely beautiful concept is modeled. The humility Jesus speaks of is not at all self-doubting, self-hating, small, or timid. It is also not boastful or arrogant.

Let's also look at Mary, the mother of Jesus. Her confident humility was in her quiet strength and steadfast faith. She was a young teenage girl and the angel of the Lord manifested himself to her one afternoon. Can you imagine this? Mary didn't boast to others, or let this incredible honor make her feel better than anyone. Mary simply obeyed and received the role He bestowed upon her.

Humility comes from knowing who we are with such an unwavering security that we are able to take the focus off ourselves and place it onto others. Humility is looking upward to Jesus, not in the mirror or to others for approval.

> *Humility is looking upward to*
> *Jesus, not in the mirror or to others*
> *for approval.*

I used to think humility meant I couldn't receive a compliment without pointing out the flaws that must have been overlooked. I used to think it meant I couldn't shine and be all I wanted to be because I might step on someone's toes. After all, I wouldn't want to do that, because then I might make someone feel uncomfortable or small. I thought humility was staying small so other people could shine.

Can you relate? In what ways has your perception of humility stopped you from stepping into the radiance of your true identity?

A woman who is humble is about Kingdom business and trusts the story God writes for her life, even if it means she will be superseded by others. She is seen by Him and knows she will never be shaken. That means she can be authentic and own her weaknesses around others. For instance, I lead a women's group and Bible study and I used to feel so much pressure to act and talk like I was an expert in every area of Christian life. But confident humility is being willing to admit your weaknesses because you know where your strength comes from. Now, our groups have a culture of sharing honestly what's going on in our lives, the good and the hard, and it's beautiful because that's where Jesus gets to show off. Do you have a group where you can safely share your true heart and life, in the midst of messy? If you don't, I'd encourage you to create or find one! Humility is being better acquainted with our own weaknesses and sins than the weaknesses and sins of someone else. Humility is quickly saying sorry when you are wrong and always saying thank you. Humility is remembering the place from which God brought you and the woman you would be without Him.

I had a real come to Jesus season with humility this year. I've always tried to stay humble so God didn't have to humble me. But apparently, I still needed a good lesson. A friend became angry at me for something. I was completely unaware of her feelings until she shunned me at a social event. She shared her feelings about me with most of our friends, which caused a lot of strife in my heart. I felt so distressed and blindsided. I didn't know if I should defend myself or just lie low. In my pain, I could feel my heart filling up with resentment and anger. My body physically began to break down from the anxiety that pierced me over the coming months.

I asked the Lord to give me eyes to see my part in hurting her. I still couldn't understand why she didn't come to me and share her feelings. I needed help in truly forgiving her for assuming the worst about me. The block was building with negative thoughts and I needed to knock it down before it festered beyond reason. One afternoon, I lay down and closed my eyes. I asked God to speak to me about how I could forgive her and bless her. Instantly, He brought to mind memories of the last five times I had hurt and betrayed Him. He also reminded me of times I hurt others. Whoa. I was undone. Who in the world was I to be shocked that someone would be unkind to me? I had absolutely no right. Immediately, it became a privilege instead of a burden to forgive my friend. Anytime I begin to judge or criticize someone in my heart, I am considering myself more highly than I ought. Could this same sentiment be blocking forgiveness in your life right now?

Paul warns us in this: "For by the grace given me I say to every one of you: Do not think of yourself more highly than you ought, but rather think of yourself with sober judgment, in accordance with the faith God has distributed to each of you" (Romans 12:3 NIV). Humility is a liberating heart posture, not a limiting one. It gives us the freedom to easily forgive, to bless, to pray for and ask God for what we can't do on our own.

A woman of humility is open to grow and learn in her gifts and character. She is always yearning to become more and more like Jesus, knowing she will never see full completion of her perfect transformation until she is celebrating with Him in Heaven. Knowing your identity in Christ leads to confidence, and knowing who you are in Christ leads to humility.

Humility = The Sparkle Effect

Prayer

Dear Father:

I want to be that girl who reveals divine humility and confidence to onlookers. I want people to see what it looks like to be so secure in You that I am not driven by self-seeking motives. Will You teach me what it means to be confidently humble? I want to embrace it and become it.

Please give me a fresh revelation when I am reading Your Words. Make them leap out at me so they are real, tangible, and relatable. God, I want to know Your love and power on such a deep level that I am led to my knees to praise your name. I would be lost without You. In You, I am found, known for all my weaknesses, and loved. Help me to be that for someone else. In Jesus' name, Amen.

Wonder Words

When pride comes, then comes disgrace, but with humility comes wisdom.

—Proverbs 11:2

Live in harmony with one another. Do not be proud, but be willing to associate with people of low position. Do not be conceited.

—Romans 12:16

Therefore, as God's chosen people, holy and dearly loved, clothe yourselves with compassion, kindness, humility, gentleness and patience.

—Colossians 3:12

Your beauty should not come from outward adornment, such as elaborate hairstyles and the wearing of gold jewelry or fine clothes. Rather, it should be that of your inner self, the unfading beauty of a gentle and quiet spirit, which is of great worth in God's sight.

—1 Peter 3:3–4

Humble yourselves before the Lord, and he will lift you up.

—James 4:10

chapter 18

Sparkle with Sincerity

I have in sincerity, pledged myself to your
service as so many of you are pledged to mine.

—*Queen Elizabeth II*

One of my final questions at Miss USA was, "What is your
definition of beauty?" Without hesitation, I answered, "Beauty is
how you make other people feel. They might not remember anything about you, but they will remember the way you made them
feel." Maya Angelou said it as well: "I've learned that people will
forget what you did. People will forget what you said, but people
will never forget how you made them feel." And it's something I
truly believe.

I was blessed to grow up in a home where we learned that
everyone mattered. I saw my parents treat everyone with kindness
whether it was the city mayor or the neighborhood garbage man.
I remember hearing my mother tell me that Princess Diana was
more than royalty; she was a people's princess. My mother had a
coffee table book filled with photos of her that I studied in awe.
She was royalty, in the highest position of status in England, but
she spent her days as a public servant visiting with refugees in

third world countries, comforting sick children in hospitals, and lifting the spirits of wounded soldiers. She won the hearts of people around the world because of the way she made them feel.

Many dignitaries do a lot of the same humanitarian work or make the same appearances that Princess Diana did, but something was different about her. Her work was not about photo ops. She put her life in danger when she traveled to Angola and walked through only a partially cleared minefield during her work with the International Campaign to Ban Landmines. She actually cared about people regardless of what they could do for her. Diana is a role model of beauty in many ways for women because of the way she treated people in strength and humility.

In Western culture, value is placed on getting ahead so our interactions with people are often minimized to networking events and business card exchanges. Our questions swirl narrowly around the primary interest of what others do... better yet, what they can do for us.

Treating people with kindness and honor, even those who seemingly can't do anything for us, is the heart of Jesus, and it shines through in all areas of our life. We will never be successful if we go through life dismissing people and selecting whom we will be kind to. Living as a daughter of God means that we are royalty, it means that our sisters and brothers in Christ are royalty, too, regardless of how they rank by the world's standards. We are called to be a people's princess.

This might seem like an easy concept: "Okay, cool. Be nice to people; got it." But it's a little deeper than that. It isn't just about how you act or what you say. Making people feel valued is really about what you believe. We can be really good at acting nicely toward someone when we're in a good mood or we are face-to-face with them, but what about instances such as when we are on the phone with customer service?

I'll be honest, I've gotten off the phone with customer service reps thinking, *Whoa, I can't believe I got so aggressive.* In those cases, it's easy to get frustrated because our patience is tested waiting on the line forever to be connected to a real person. Once they're on the line, we can dismiss them as a robot, especially since they communicate in scripted responses the entire phone call.

Kris has been the best example to me. The other day, I heard him for three hours on the phone with a customer service rep. The rep was definitely grating on my nerves because she wasn't being efficient and it was majorly delaying Kris's plans for the day. But he was so kind to her. He talked to her the exact same way he would talk to one of his clients. Even speaking to someone over the phone we will never meet can be an opportunity to show them they are valuable, and to practice radiant character.

The way Kris handled that phone call reminded me of how Jesus sees us. We are all royal in His sight. Whether or not they can do anything for anyone, the poorest person will be many times richer in eternal life than the richest man on earth who didn't love God.

Jesus taught a lesson about a rich young man who chose worldly wealth over the Kingdom. He said, "And everyone who has left houses or brothers or sisters or father or mother or children or farms for My name's sake, will receive many times as much, and will inherit eternal life. But many who are first will be last; and the last, first" (Matthew 19:30 NIV). When faced with the choice, the rich man chose to follow wealth over Jesus. We won't be faced with such a drastic choice every day. But Jesus makes the point that when we sincerely care for other people by following Him, we will be taken care of in all the other ways.

Here is how to engage your sincerity to make people feel like royalty:

1. Ask God to help you see people through His eyes.

As the writer of 1 Samuel put it, "For the LORD sees not as man sees: man looks on the outward appearance, but the LORD looks on the heart" (16:17 ESV).

I have prayed specifically for God to help me see people the way He sees them. I knew I couldn't minister to people if I didn't understand them or have compassion for them. I remember the first person I began seeing through God's eyes. It was someone who seemed to always have an issue or conflict with others. Through my own eyes, I saw she was opinionated, loud, extremely sensitive, and talked about herself. Before the next time I saw her, I prayed and asked God to give me eyes to see her the way He did. As we sat together and talked, a tenderness came over me for her. She was the same as usual, but I saw something different, something deeper. I saw her little girl heart; I could feel her pain and understand her intentions. I felt a grace come into my heart to hear her out, make her feel loved and known. I remember coming home on such a high! I thought, *What a different world we would live in if we all saw each other through God's eyes? It's like a superpower!*

You can do that with people, too, even someone you don't naturally vibe with. All you have to do is pray to have eyes to truly see them.

We tend to judge what we don't understand. It's much nicer going through life seeing through God's lens rather than our own. This is the kind of prayer God wants to answer, so believe that He will open the eyes of your heart to see as He does. It's fun for you and can be life changing for others.

2. Show no partiality among the rich and the poor.

This verse says it all:

> My brothers, show no partiality as you hold the faith in
> our Lord Jesus Christ, the Lord of glory. For if a man wear-
> ing a gold ring and fine clothing comes into your assembly,
> and a poor man in shabby clothing also comes in, and if
> you pay attention to the one who wears the fine clothing
> and say, "You sit here in a good place," while you say to
> the poor man, "You stand over there," or, "Sit down at my
> feet," have you not then made distinctions among your-
> selves and become judges with evil thoughts? Listen, my
> beloved brothers, has not God chosen those who are poor
> in the world to be rich in faith and heirs of the king-
> dom, which he has promised to those who love him? (James
> 2:1–3 ESV)

3. Pay attention to your line of questioning.

Make an effort to ask people about anything other than about
what they do. Ask questions that address the heart like, "What
makes you laugh? What makes you cry? What do you dream
about? What are you excited about this year?" These three questions alone will open up a world of depth in a person. That's
when we make sincere connections with people! Connecting with
someone on a heart level rather than a transactional level is where
the gold is. Be the person who finds the gold.

4. Remember names and something special about them.

When you meet someone, repeat their name and use it when appropriate throughout the conversation. There is power in saying someone's name and shows them they are important enough for you to be engaged. Starbucks understands this importance. The barista always asks for your name and calls it out when your order is ready. The really good ones ask for the spelling. Doesn't it feel good to see your name correctly spelled out? That's one subconscious reason people become regular customers. At other restaurants, you are an order number. When we identify ourselves with companies, offices, or institutions, we give our birth date or social security number. In a world where we are reduced to numbers, be a woman who calls out a name. Remember at least one special thing about them so you can bring it up the next time you see them.

5. Listen.

You might have heard your mama say that God gave us two ears and one mouth so we could listen twice as much as we talk. We don't often get the chance to express our thoughts and feelings, so when you give someone a chance to open up, it's refreshing. Resist the urge to use something they say as a cue to start talking about yourself. Here's an example:

Friend: "I went to Hawaii last weekend!"
You: "Really? I went there last summer and stayed at the Four Seasons. It was the best trip of our lives. We went snorkeling and deep-sea diving with all of our best friends. I think we're going back in a few months!"

Do you know someone who hijacks your excitement like this? How does it make you feel?

Many people feel like this is a good way to relate to the other person. In reality, it's like taking a pin to their balloon. Instead, if a friend shares something with you, ask sincere follow-up questions to show that you are genuinely interested and allow your friend to have their moment to shine.

6. See Jesus in everyone.

As Jesus said, "Whatever you did not do for one of the least of these, you did not do for me" (Matthew 25:45).

Jesus tells us that rejecting or overlooking people when they need something is the same thing as rejecting Jesus Himself. When we encounter someone in need, we may tend to look the other way if we feel uncomfortable. Maybe it's a homeless person asking for money, maybe it's someone in a wheelchair, or maybe it's that girl who sits alone at lunch. At least make eye contact and acknowledge you see them. Even if you don't have anything to give, remember that every brokenhearted or downcast person you meet is God's child. You have an opportunity to love God by loving them.

On the flip side, remember to see the Jesus in mean, prideful people, too. No one acts superior or cold unless they've been hurt and are trying to compensate for the pain. Just like the rain falls on the righteous and the wicked alike, we must also bless those who are difficult to bless. This is being like God.

Jesus reminds us to "love your enemies, bless those who curse you, do good to those who hate you, and pray for those who spitefully use you and persecute you, that you may be sons of your Father in Heaven; for He makes His sun rise on the evil and on the good, and sends rain on the just and on the unjust. For if you love those who love you, what reward have you? Do not even the tax collectors do the same?" (Matthew 5:44–46 NKJV).

7. Encourage and compliment others.

Words are a gift and have the power to shift the course of an entire life. Encouraging can be as simple as commenting on something beautiful and positive about a person, and there are so many opportunities to do it daily. Take time to notice the cashier at the grocery store or the barista at the coffee shop. Too many of us keep our eyes on our phones and barely utter a word. Be the one who takes time to lift your eyes up. Complimenting someone doesn't cost you anything, but words are priceless. You may be the only kindness they experience in a long time. You will be surprised how lifting up others will refresh your own spirit as well.

I often write little notes to people I meet throughout the day. That way they can hold on to the note and read it over again. One time, I was on the elliptical at the gym. I looked around, asking the Lord whom He wanted to speak to. He highlighted a girl on a treadmill with headphones on. Nothing about her externally suggested she was sad, but I sensed it. I ended my workout and went to write her a note detailing what I felt God wanted to say. I dropped it off on her treadmill. She was certainly a little confused and maybe even uncomfortable. But that was okay with me; I decided to just be obedient to God and let Him take care of the rest.

A little over a year later, I was at the gym again in the weight room. A girl approached me and said, "You're Kristen, right?" I said, "Yes," not realizing who she was. "I'm Ashley [name changed for discretion]. You wrote me a note and gave it to me here over a year ago. I just wanted to tell you it changed my life. I've started to realize my self-worth and left an abusive relationship."

Most of the time, you will have no idea how you impacted someone. Rarely do we get such sweet moments affirming the way we've touched someone. I knew God gave me that moment to remind me to keep loving the unreached whether we get a response or not.

A queen is an encourager. "Let no corrupting talk come out of your mouth, but only such as is good for building up, as fits the occasion, that it may give grace to those who hear" (Ephesians 4:29 ESV).

8. Treat others the way you want to be treated.

We all know the Golden Rule: Treat others how we want to be treated. I know there are occasions I need this reminder. The Gospel of Matthew states, "So whatever you wish that others would do to you, do also to them, for this is the Law and the Prophets" (7:12 ESV).

God gives and takes away. Nothing truly belongs to us. It's important to remember that we could lose all we have at any point and need someone to lean on. Proverbs 27:10 says, "Never abandon a friend—either yours or your father's" (NLT). When disaster strikes, you won't have to ask your brother for assistance. Be there for someone when they need help.

9. Cover one another.

The way we treat people behind their backs is arguably more important than the way we treat them to their face. Proverbs says that a gossip causes division, which is the agenda of the devil (16:28). Isn't that crazy to think about? It's not a lighthearted thing girls do. Gossip is partnering with the devil. When someone wrongs us, we want our friends to take our side, which is one of the reasons we itch to gossip. We also like to gossip because we think it makes us look better by making the other person worse. When we feel threatened, gossip is an attempt to control our image and rally the allegiance of others. But Proverbs 16:7 promises, "When the way you live pleases the Lord, he makes even your enemies live at peace with you" (NIV).

10. Outdo one another in honor.

The New Testament tells us to "Love one another with brotherly affection. Outdo one another in showing honor" (Romans 12:10 ESV).

It is so awesome to get the chance to honor people who make our lives better in any capacity. Whether it's a speaker who just gave an awesome message, our husband who works hard, or a family member or friend who loves you well. Honoring them is doing something that makes them feel special. As always, the Bible calls us to outdo each other in honor. People don't get recognized enough; our talents and gifts aren't called out enough. When we honor each other, we are honoring our Creator. Make honoring others a game by constantly trying to outdo them with thoughtfulness!

On the day of my rehearsal dinner for my wedding, Kris and I decided to use that time to honor our bridal party, our planner, and our families. Our friends and family put so much into wedding preparation and all the festivities leading up to it and I didn't take it lightly. Kris and I had gifts and a handwritten letter for each person who helped us and we publicly acknowledged them for what they meant to us and why.

Treating other people well, especially when it is unexpected, unnoticed, or difficult is part of stepping into the radiance of your true identity every day.

Making people feel valuable isn't going to come from completing items on a checklist. Politicians can do that. People can see through it. Everything good originates in the heart, and if you are sincere, people will feel your warmth.

Consider these questions:

Is there anything blocking you from sincerity?

Who could you encourage today?

How can you cover someone in love who maybe doesn't deserve it?

Where is God calling you to ask some thoughtful questions and listen more carefully?

> *Everything good originates in the heart, and if you are sincere, people will feel your warmth.*

Sincerity = The Sparkle Effect

Prayer

Dear Father:

I want to reflect Your love in every situation I am in. God, please strengthen me to be calm and kind when my patience is tested. Please help me to guard my mouth so only uplifting and productive words flow into the hearts of others. God, I want to be sincere. Open my eyes to see past myself and to be secure enough in You that I can be truly focused on others. You are the ultimate encourager; please help me to be sincerely encouraging.

Gossiping is something I struggle with, Lord. I admit, gossiping feels satisfying in the moment, but I feel guilty later. Help me to trust You and realize I don't need to gossip to get people on my side. Father, I know I am royalty, but help me to be a people's princess so I can give a foretaste of Heaven to all I encounter. Amen.

Wonder Words

Don't rejoice when your enemies fall;
don't be happy when they stumble.
For the Lord will be displeased with you
and will turn his anger away from them.
                              —Proverbs 24:17–18

This is my commandment: Love each other in the same way I have loved you.
                              —John 15:12

Don't look out only for your own interests, but take an interest in others, too.
                              —Philippians 2:4

Since God chose you to be the holy people he loves, you must clothe yourselves with tenderhearted mercy, kindness, humility, gentleness, and patience. Make allowance for each other's faults, and forgive anyone who offends you. Remember, the Lord forgave you, so you must forgive others.
                              —Colossians 3:12–13

If someone says, "I love God," but hates a fellow believer, that person is a liar; for if we don't love people we can see, how can we love God, whom we cannot see? And he has given us this command: Those who love God must also love their fellow believers.

—1 John 4:20–21

chapter 19

Sparkle with Purity

Now, think the happiest of things. It's the same
as having wings.

—*Peter Pan*

Blessed are the pure in heart, for they will see God"
(Matthew 5:8 NIV).

The more we detox our lives from un-Godly stimuli, the more
sensitive to it we become. On the flip side, the more darkness
we expose our minds to, the more immune and tolerant to it we
become. Just because something becomes acceptable or tolerated
does not make it pure or lovely. A queen doesn't simply do what
is accepted, she does what's respected.

I used to listen to pop radio all day, every day, and not feel affected by the lyrics, at least consciously. I could watch *Law and
Order: SVU* and *Criminal Minds* without having nightmares. But
once I started tuning more into God's channel and tuning out impure channels, things changed.

When Kris and I started dating, I learned he didn't watch TV.
I was concerned he might not approve of my DVR list of *Mil-
lionaire Matchmaker*, *The Bachelor*, *Revenge*, and *The Real Housewives*

and wondered if he was a little strange. *Who doesn't watch TV and why? Unless you have extreme beliefs or don't have electricity?*

About three months into our relationship, I noticed I hadn't turned on my TV once. Life with him kept me busy and social. I decided to save some money and cancel my cable. If I really wanted to watch a show, I could watch it online. But that didn't work because when I went online to look up a show, it made me recognize the effort I was putting in to watch a show when I could be using that effort for something better. So I just stopped watching TV altogether, and now it has been six years of a TV-free life—aside from movie nights.

One day, as we were choosing a movie to watch from our Netflix account, I realized it had TV shows, too. Oh, how I had missed my *Bachelor* and *Revenge*. If only I could watch one episode of Emily Thorne masterfully kicking butt and framing someone else. And then I saw that I could watch all the seasons of *Revenge*! Oh, how wonderful!

What started out as watching just one episode turned into binge-watching multiple seasons in a few days. Kris watched some of the first ones with me, but then he went out of town and I watched too many by myself in the daytime and at night. I noticed my thoughts darkening. I felt more aggressive and depressed. I even started imagining myself as Emily Thorne getting revenge on the people in my life who hurt me. I knew I had to stop watching the show. I went online and looked up what happened in the very end so I wouldn't be tempted to watch any more.

Purity is relevant and necessary in your life because it's about honoring and protecting the connection you have with God, your dreams, your peace, your mind, and your heart. Purity isn't just about sexuality. It's about keeping your head and heart clear from anything that will give the enemy an opening to lead you into a downward spiral.

> *Purity is relevant and necessary in your life because it's about honoring and protecting the connection you have with God, your dreams, your peace, your mind, and your heart.*

In the United States, we are especially susceptible to negativity because of social media, TV, pop culture, magazines, and all the comparison that comes from engaging it. There are many deadly "channels" masked in alluring coverings just vying for our purity.

The enemy is crafty. He is disguised as an angel of light. He isn't obvious and apparent. But if we are protecting our purity, we can discern a distraction at the onset rather than when it's too late. The enemy can use a good thing, like fun music or a popular TV show, to distract us from our path, our calling, and our relationship with Jesus. That "good thing" can influence our thoughts and our moods, and can cloud our spiritual state. Have you ever gone to a party or watched a movie and felt dark or icky afterward? Opening the shiny door to the popular thing can lead to an array of impure things.

A good or popular thing doesn't necessarily mean it's a God-thing. If we let even a good thing like a dream or a relationship consume us, it can fog our queenly perspective. If we devote so much to that good thing, it can become the center of our life. When it rules us, we may compromise for it. And suddenly, that good thing or person has control over us. That is when it isn't good anymore. If you're honest with yourself, does something that was once a good thing have too much control over you now?

One season, I noticed the enemy has been using my desire to accomplish goals to distract me from my main purpose. I was spending so much time sending e-mails, finishing small projects, and focusing on my modeling career that I was neglecting my primary calling—to write and speak. The enemy knows my weakness for immediate gratification and disguises it as a good thing. I get energized by the results I get from hustling and booking a job. Booking a commercial can happen sooner and quicker than writing a book. The enemy feeds my lack of focus. He doesn't want me to finish this book that could change a heart and release a daughter's radiance. What good things are drawing your attention away from a God-thing?

The enemy's tactics are so covert that I didn't even notice my mission had been compromised until three weeks later. I like to consider myself discerning, but I was thrown off. I had to refocus my prayer and heart back on God's mission. I had to peel myself away from my in-box and away from my phone. I had to stick headphones in my ears and play worship music to block out my own distracting thoughts so I could get back to writing. I had to create in myself a clean heart again.

How is the enemy sneaking into your pure head and heart space? How is he diverting your attention away from God and His purpose for you?

The best way to identify an obstruction to your purity is to identify the culprit taking priority over God. Is it a person? Is it social media? Is it the need to be liked? Is it TV? Is it food or alcohol? We are sensitive to external stimuli more than we think. It's important to guard ourselves in order to protect the pure radiance within us.

Here are six areas that are necessary and relevant to protecting your purity:

1. Watch.

In regard to negative TV content, *Psychology Today* states, "TV watchers are more likely to feel anxious, unsafe and fear personal violence in their daily life." If you don't think TV affects your thoughts, feelings, and mood, try not watching for a week and then watch again. When you purify your mind and then expose it to trash again, you will feel it. Imagine how the visual images are affecting your subconscious mind.

2. Listen.

The lyrics and spirit behind the music you listen to can inspire and soothe you or irritate and aggravate you. The more exposure to songs with degrading lyrics, the more desensitized you become. Just because a song promotes promiscuity doesn't mean it's what a real man wants. And it definitely doesn't lead to fulfillment because it isn't what we were made for.

3. Read.

One of my weaknesses is comparing myself to others. Social media makes this a constant temptation because it's addicting to scroll its pages. I've made it a goal not to scroll more than ten minutes a day, and I specifically don't look at profiles that may trigger feelings of comparison. Instead of jumping on Instagram in the morning, read a chapter from a spiritual book, download the Bible App, journal, go on a walk, meditate, or read a devotional. The way you start your day directs the course of your day.

4. Consume.

In the same way our media consumption can benefit or harm us, the things we eat and drink have a direct correlation on our moods, energy level, and mental clarity. That bag of chips might be easy to eat, but it's going to cause you to crash later. The best way to manage what you eat is to plan ahead. A queen plans ahead. Make sure your fridge is stocked with produce and protein to make salads or wraps. Have a bowl of cut up fruit to graze on through the day. Pack your lunches or stash healthy snacks in your car, like almonds and Lara Bars. When life gets really busy, I can easily neglect going to the grocery store or forget to pack healthy snacks for a long drive.

If you notice your mood is slipping, you've been feeling depressed or irritable; take inventory of your diet and how often you eat throughout the day. Make sure you are eating every 2–3 hours to keep your blood sugar up. It's wise to get your bloodwork done once a year to find out if you are deficient in any area in which you can compensate with vitamins.

5. Set sexual boundaries.

Your body was created to be a temple in which the presence of God lives. It is a treasure. When you really believe in your value, you will realize the power you have in holding the key to your sexual purity. God has given us statutes to help protect, not limit, His daughters from regret, diseases, and shame.

God's will is for you to be set apart for him in holiness and that you keep yourselves unpolluted from sexual defilement (1 Thessalonians 4:3).

I've been a part of several conversations with women who have a completely different view of female sexual empowerment. Their general belief is that women are empowered when they are sexually active, however, and with as many men as they want. I can understand this viewpoint in light of such harsh oppression of women around the world. In some cultures, women are stoned, arrested, or killed if they have sex before or outside marriage. But do you believe that sleeping around leads to personal freedom?

In general, there is no such thing as no strings attached. Sex releases a hormone called oxytocin in a woman's body, which is known as the bonding hormone. It's the same hormone released when a mother is nursing that bonds her and her baby to each other. Protect yourself from bonding your body and soul to someone who isn't your husband. You are worthy of protecting your body from an unnecessary bond to someone who won't be bound to you in covenant.

6. Forgive.

One of the most powerful things you can do to preserve your sparkle is forgive quickly. The moment you become aware of hurt and anger creeping in, do whatever it takes to let them go. Unforgiveness is toxic and will spread faster than you realize and start to control you. I've heard it said that unforgiveness is like drinking poison and expecting the other person to die. It doesn't protect you from getting hurt again; it only hurts you. Forgive so you will experience freedom and make sure the enemy doesn't have an open wound on which to infect you.

Take inventory of your life. Be on the defensive against negative incoming influencers. Only you know who those are for you. For me, they are certain people who make me feel small when I spend time with them. Recognize the people or areas that trigger you and put boundaries in place. Create a space for the Holy Spirit to thrive by keeping a clean heart. The more you are filled with Godly things, like peace, goodness, and joy, the less you will want of the counterfeits.

It's imperative to maintain a pure heart if you want to be the queen of your life living on purpose to expand the Kingdom of God.

Purity = The Sparkle Effect

Prayer

Dear Father:

I want to be close to You. I want to be pure in my heart so I can tap into Your voice, so I can see what You see and say what You say. Lord, everything in this life is meaningless if You are not at the center. Please help me to recognize where the enemy might attack me. Show me where I am weak, where I am susceptible of a good thing turning into a distraction and an idol.

God, please give me the desire and discipline to pull away from the people or influences in my life that are clouding my mind and heart. I want my channels to be open and clear for Your voice. There is nothing that compares with the euphoria and power of Heaven. Will You give me tastes of it? Nothing would be sweeter to me. You make me whole; You give me meaning; You make me redeemed, treasured, and loved. Help me to be a vessel who hosts Your presence because of my purity. Amen.

Wonder Words

To the pure you show yourself pure, but to the wicked you show yourself hostile.

—Psalm 18:26

Behold, You desire truth in the innermost being, And in the hidden part You will make me know wisdom.

—Psalm 51:6

Your eyes are too pure to look on evil; you cannot tolerate wrongdoing.

—Habbakuk 1:13

Therefore consider the members of your earthly body as dead to immorality, impurity, passion, evil desire, and greed, which amounts to idolatry.

—Colossians 3:5

chapter 20

Sparkle with Wisdom

At the age of nineteen, you always think you
are prepared for everything and you always
think you have the knowledge for what's
coming ahead.

—*Princess Diana*

It can be frustrating listening to a talk or a message on God's
great purpose and dream for our lives when we feel confused as to
what our purpose even is. Maybe you have felt a little frustrated
even going through this book! I'm proud of you for being persistent. We may have the faint vision of what we want to be, but
nothing in our life, not even our own skill set, is ready for it yet.

Maybe you feel like you aren't good at anything. Or maybe
you feel like you're pretty good at a lot of things. I had a hard
time narrowing down exactly what I was made for because I have
a skill set and interest in several areas. In high school, I loved performing in musical theater, singing, acting, and political debate.
The reason my dream of becoming Miss USA was a constant for
me is partly because I could combine almost all my interests in
that job. I figured I could be Miss USA for a year and that would
help me decide what to do next.

When I moved to Los Angeles, I still didn't have a clear career direction so I set my sights on TV hosting because I knew I could do it well. I took hosting classes, got a hosting agent, made a reel, took film/TV classes for acting, secured a theatrical manager, went on auditions, and booked some jobs in those first few years. I was modeling and doing commercials, which were great, but it didn't fulfill me. The feeling of emptiness and frustration set in because I wasn't operating in my purpose. I was doing things I enjoyed and am good at, but it wasn't my calling. I felt a bit aimless.

In the meantime, I began pursuing a deeper relationship with God again. The more God revealed who He was to me, the more I felt the burning desire to share what He was saying with other young women, too.

One day, I had an *aha* moment. It was one of those moments you see a montage of memories in a few seconds. I saw all my life events, strengths, passions, and interests blend together. I felt this deep longing to inspire women in the same way God had inspired me.

As I've mentioned, Joyce Meyer had a huge impact on my life. I love how candidly she speaks, how unapologetically true she is to the Word, and how she ministers around the world. Just like Miss USA had been my childhood role model, Joyce Meyer became my new role model. Joyce's words go straight to my heart and I want to communicate just as effectively.

Through prayer and the inspiration others gave me, God finally revealed to me that my calling was to combine my gift of performing and communicating with my passion for God and women. I sensed a resounding *yes* in my spirit. I would answer the call.

After years of wondering, I finally knew my purpose—but *now what?* I came up with a plan of how I was going to implement my vision and it started with writing through my personal blog. I sat down at the computer and readied my fingers over the keyboard.

Nothing came. There was a block, like a wall up. Nothing was coming. Nothing was flowing. I felt discouraged and confused. I knew what my purpose was, but now I needed to do it! Why couldn't I?

Does this resonate? Do you feel like you know what you were made for—do you have that certainty—but you feel like you don't know where or how to begin? And even when you do, it feels like there is resistance?

In my despair, I returned to Joyce Meyer and read a devotional that talked about seasons, specifically seasons of preparation. I had never heard of this concept before. There are seasons, like the winter, where we have to hibernate so God can grow us, teach us, prune us, and prepare us for the next step. He loves us too much to let us launch too quickly into something we aren't ready for. We may think we are ready, but God knows best. Of course, we will never fully arrive until the day we meet Jesus, but there is a certain level of preparedness that needs to be in place before God graduates us from the training ground. After reading Joyce's devotional, I did some more research into this concept.

God says that He will hide us in the shadow of His wings to protect us. He may be hiding you right now, just like a flower hides in the winter for protection so it can bloom again in the spring.

It is crucial for our success and well-being to understand there are different seasons we go through. The Book of Ecclesiastes says there is a time for everything under the sun. You may be in a season of preparation right now. If not, there will be a time that you do go into one, so don't dismay.

God couldn't launch me into speaking and writing until my character was refined to match the task. I still had a lot of preparing to do, not only in my character, but in my knowledge and understanding of His nature and the Word.

God took me into a long season of studying the Word, journaling, reading faith inspiration books, and participating in Bible studies with wiser, older women.

In what ways do you need to grow? What things can you do now to prepare you for what you want to step into?

As a daughter of the King, you have the desire to have meaning and purpose. You were made for it. You may get down on yourself because you don't feel the peace to move on it yet, but that is because you are probably in a season of preparation. Give yourself grace and be willing to open your eyes to see the areas in your life in which God wants to grow you.

When I learned more about spiritual seasons, it gave me permission to relax and effectively engage in a season of preparation. Finally, one day as I was praying, I felt Him lift the wall and say, "GO." I raced to my laptop and logged into my blog account to begin writing. The words began to flow from my mind through my fingertips onto the computer screen. He had released me into the next step of His purpose.

Since then, there have definitely been seasons when He brings me back to be quiet and to work out a roadblock or challenge. It can be discouraging, but now that I understand seasons, I'm able to release the urge to resist or steam ahead. I know I need to be quenched like the flowers in April showers or retreat into hibernation like bears in the winter.

Be aware of what season you are in and give yourself the grace to be there. Seek God's wisdom to discern your purpose and partner with Him to get there. The more in tune you are with how God works and what He is doing, the more quickly you will be able to get in step with Him and abide in peace.

Seek God's wisdom to discern your purpose and partner with Him to get there.

What season are you in?

What does God want to work out in you?

In what areas do you want breakthrough?

Make a list of potential mentors.

Is there a group of older, wiser women you could join?

God loves you too much to launch you into something you aren't ready for. In the meantime, seek wisdom—God will give it without measure.

Wisdom = The Sparkle Effect

Prayer

Dear Father:

Thank You for the purpose You have predestined for my life. Lord, I have the longing to expand and glorify Your Kingdom. I want You to use me, but I also want to bring honor to Your name. Lord, thank You so much for protecting me. Thank You so much for seasons, because they are for my good. I don't always like change, but I know that I will not fully partake in Your splendor if I don't embrace change. Please show me what season I am in and grant me the ability to trust You as You grow me. God, show me when it is time to rest, time to act, and time to prepare. Thank You for loving me enough to protect me when I am not ready to act. In Jesus' name, Amen.

Wonder Words

He changes times and seasons; he removes kings and sets up kings; he gives wisdom to the wise and knowledge to those who have understanding.

—Daniel 2:21

And let us not grow weary of doing good, for in due season we will reap, if we do not give up.

—Galatians 6:9

While the earth remains, seedtime and harvest, cold and heat, summer and winter, day and night, shall not cease.

—Genesis 8:22

He is like a tree planted by streams of water that yields its fruit in its season, and its leaf does not wither. In all that he does, he prospers.

—Psalm 1:3

For everything there is a season, and a time for every matter under heaven.

—Ecclesiastes 3:1

chapter 21

Sparkle with Right Motives

Do small things with great love.

—*Mother Teresa*

When Kris and I started dating, he took me up to a church called Bethel. I remember looking it up online and being a little skeptical when I read about the "signs and wonders" and "glory clouds of gold dust" that manifested there. I had never heard of a church like this before. *Was it even biblical?* I learned Bethel is a place where people operate in the gifts of the Spirit. The gift of prophecy is one of them. Until this, I had never experienced or even really understood what the gifts of the Spirit were and if we could partake in them. I grew up in Protestant churches which were marvelous in biblical teaching, but I didn't learn about spiritual gifts.

If you are like me and this is new to you, let me quickly shed light on what the Bible says about the gift of prophecy: "Pursue love, and earnestly desire the spiritual gifts, especially that you may prophesy" (1 Corinthians 14:1 ESV). We are all called to *especially* seek the gift of prophecy. It might sound like a word you associate with psychics, fortune-tellers, or palm readers. But prophecy isn't about reading minds or telling futures. Prophecy is listening to what God is saying, looking at a person through His perspective, and then speaking a word over that person for the purpose of uplifting and edifying. As 1 Corinthians 14:3 tells us, "The one who prophesies speaks to people for their upbuilding and encouragement and consolation" (ESV).

On my first visit to Bethel, I timidly followed Kris into the sanctuary. Not long after, three girls around my age came up to me and asked if they could pray for me. I'd never had anyone stop me to pray over me before. I was intrigued and ready to receive anything God had for me so I said yes. They began to speak destiny and life over me. This was the first time I had experienced anything like this, but somehow I wasn't afraid or nervous. I felt total peace. As they prayed, hot, healing tears rolled down my cheeks.

The words that impacted me the most were, "You are a Queen Esther in the Spirit." I loved the story of Esther in the Bible. She was a strong woman of prayer, wisdom, and action. She was an ordinary girl who was placed into a royal position for a massive purpose. She was born for such a time as this, and in her bravery to the call, she saved an entire race of people.

This young prayer warrior told me I was born to do something great like Esther. I felt on top of the world after that. I felt special.

But since that moment, I have heard many other young women told that they are a Queen Esther, too. The first time it happened, I cringed. I thought, *Umm no. I am Queen Esther...you clearly are not hearing from God correctly.* Have you ever felt annoyed when it feels someone else has swerved into your lane? Or that you aren't unique like you thought?

I'm chuckling as I reflect on that moment and many others just like it. I can laugh now because God has done some humbling, but much needed work in me. Now I see the immature, insecure girl I was. I feel compassion for the insecure girl in me because she was just trying to find her place in the world. I was confused as to how each person is created uniquely yet shares the same anointing as someone else. Maybe you are trying to find your place in the world, too.

Have you ever felt that way? That you are excited for the things God wants to accomplish through you, but you lose focus on building and measuring success. Just because we are doing something good for God doesn't mean our motive is pure. No matter what space we are in, even ministry, the need to be recognized for doing something great can still creep in.

Even though I had a good heart and wanted to do good for other young women by starting my ministry, I still had the desire to be known for it. The desire to be widely acknowledged can destroy our impact, but mostly our joy.

Shortly after I started *She Is More,* God had been so fun in giving me amazing ideas for the blog. I began featuring my friends' stories on the website and eventually formed a group of regular contributors. The site was taking off and getting over a million impressions monthly. As I shared before, I noticed blogs and Instagram accounts started popping up like mine. One in particular really bothered me. I felt that fiery feeling in my stomach when you find out someone copied you. I always justified that being copied is like someone stealing a part of you, so why wouldn't it make me mad? I secretly wished these blogs would fail or go away. I wasn't supportive and didn't share their content. All the while, my blog was supposedly about empowering women. But that was only if they weren't competing with me. If I were really about Kingdom business and purely wanted to help girls realize their true identity, then what was my problem with other girls doing the same?

What motivates you to do the things you do?

When we aren't secure in our identity as God's daughter, our right motives can be tainted. The moment our motives deviate from God's motives, we are susceptible to defining our success by the wrong things and being unhappy doing them.

> *The moment our motives deviate from God's motives, we are susceptible to defining our success by the wrong things.*

Our motives can't be about results, fame, money, approval, validation, competing, winning, or beating others. And Ecclesiastes 1:1–5 helps us remember that chasing fame, wealth, and comfort in this life is ultimately meaningless.

"Meaningless! Meaningless!"
says the Teacher.
"Utterly meaningless!
Everything is meaningless."
What do people gain from all their labors
at which they toil under the sun?
Generations come and generations go,
but the earth remains forever.
The sun rises and the sun sets,
and hurries back to where it rises. (NIV)

Our motives usually start out pure. Something stirs in our hearts to do something meaningful out of our own experience or pain. It's during the process of carrying out our ideas that our motives can get skewed. We become tempted by the promise of progress, growth, and notoriety. Nothing feels good about throwing a pity party when someone surpasses you or you are overlooked. The truth is, being overlooked or surpassed is going to happen in life, so you might as well figure out a way to beat self-pity. You can have a new knee jerk reaction to it. True freedom is being genuinely happy for someone and cheering even your competitors on.

Here are five ways to be successful even when you are overlooked:

1. Keep a heavenly focus.

Sometimes people beat us, copy us, and get more recognition even when it isn't deserved. Sometimes we pour into people who end up surpassing us. I have mentored girls who have exceeded me. It used to really bother me, but then I learned that is exactly how it's supposed to be. If our motives aren't God's motives, then we will get defeated, get jealous, feel wronged, and get burned out. Queens do not feel jealous when another girl succeeds because she is confident in her leadership and longevity in the Kingdom. When we focus on storing up treasures in Heaven, we will remain steadfast in the ebb and flow of what's happening in this life, whether it is good or bad. Ask God to show you what His motivations are for the thing He has called you to. You may need to ask him many times through the course of your life to get refocused again.

We start seeing the competitors around us and get scared that they will take something away from us. The thing is, they might get bigger than you, or they might get more attention than you. Someone else carrying out the same call as you is only a problem if you forget that you are in the Kingdom and the Kingdom is within you.

2. We don't have to be afraid.

What is the root of our aspiration to get ahead? Why do we feel like resources are scarce? The fact is, Darwin's theory of evolution depicts our basic instinct to survive. He says, "Those who are weak in body and mind will soon be eliminated." We may not be living in the jungle fighting for food and shelter, but we are in a different kind of jungle fighting for our survival in our careers, which has a direct effect on our well-being.

Thankfully for Jesus, His death and resurrection conquered scarcity and gave us access to unlimited resources. We have freedom when we take the focus off ourselves and pray that God will give us the pure desire to expand the Kingdom, even if it means never getting recognized.

3. God's Kingdom can't be shaken.

Have you been totally shut down after you put yourself out there? Maybe it was confusing because you thought you heard God's voice and were being obedient. For instance, when I was producing and hosting a TV show, I got to secure my own guests. There was one guest in particular I really wanted to book. I reached out to her assistant and got her all confirmed. I was so excited! The day before shooting, her assistant e-mailed me to cancel. I tried booking her again, but she wasn't available on our shoot day. Some time went by. Then one evening, I heard her speak at an event where she reminded everyone to be persistent and to keep asking and knocking on the road to our goal. I took this as a pretty clear sign I was supposed to try booking her as a guest on my show again. Obviously, I really looked up to and admired her. After a few more times trying to book her, her assistant finally told me she was too busy the rest of the year. I was disappointed. But I was surprised I didn't feel embarrassed or even resentful of her. I wasn't even mad. If I would have been let down like this before by someone I looked up to, I would have unfollowed and unliked them. But in this case, my heart was in the right place. My motives were that I wanted to share her inspiring message on my platform with more people. I thought this was a God-idea, but it simply wasn't the right timing. Either that, or I wasn't the right fit for her. That's okay, too.

When you are driven by Kingdom motives, the rejection or dismissal by people will be like water off your back.

The Kingdom can't be shaken. Remember, her turndown isn't God's final word.

4. God's promises are for everyone.

Not only does the Word promise we don't need to worry about people getting ahead of us, but Jesus is the only and best promise we need. Before Jesus came, we didn't have the promise or the hope of eternal life in Heaven. The fear of death was real so the fight for survival was brutal. But now the same power that raised Jesus from the dead lives within us.

It's important for us to remember that God can accomplish what He needs to accomplish without us. We are important and special to Him, but we aren't so important that we will be the only person assigned with our call. He is asking us to join the adventure with Him. Usually that means collaborating with and supporting other people doing what we are doing, too.

5. We have to be about God's business so He can make our business His business.

Our agenda has to be God's agenda. Even in the small things of life like meeting people at an event or interacting with your friends. Do you show up because you want something from some-one? His agenda isn't to build your kingdom; it's to build His. Remembering that alone will take the pressure off from trying to make it happen all on your own. He is more than able to accomplish the dream He placed in your heart. So, don't be busy trying to take other people down. You don't have to be the biggest and the best; you just have to be your best within the grace God has given you. For instance, I had to realize I didn't need to be the top women's inspiration blog or best writer or speaker. All I need to be concerned about is if I'm doing my best within the parameters God has allowed me.

Where God guides, He provides. He cares much more about accomplishing His vision than you do. All you have to do is say YES and stay in your own lane.

Right Motives = The Sparkle Effect

Prayer

Dear Father:

Please help me to think beyond myself. Help me to only care about Your agenda. Change my heart and help my motives be only about joining Your team to expand Your Kingdom. Lord, I want to surrender my need to be seen, known, celebrated, appreciated, and validated. I don't need any of that from people because You are the only one whose approval matters.

Father, please help me to realize that someone else's call doesn't take away from mine. Help me to let go of my fear that I will lose if I add value to their mission, especially when it is similar to mine.

God, I want to feel joy in collaborating with people rather than the threat in competing with them. Lord, help me to only care about storing up treasures in Heaven, rather than accolades on earth that will only be destroyed. I ask all of this in Jesus' name, Amen.

Wonder Words

Do not wear yourself out to get rich; do not trust your own cleverness.

—Proverbs 23:4

Do not store up for yourselves treasures on earth, where moth and rust destroy, and where thieves break in and steal. But store up for yourselves treasures in heaven, where neither moth nor rust destroys, and where thieves do not break in or steal.

—Matthew 6:19

But seek first the kingdom of God and his righteousness, and all these things will be added to you.

—Matthew 6:33

Go therefore and make disciples of all nations, baptizing them in the name of the Father and of the Son and of the Holy Spirit.

—Matthew 28:19

chapter 22

Sparkle with Enjoyment

In every job that must be done, there is an
element of fun.

—*Mary Poppins*

Life is a gift from God, even if it feels like a curse at times. It
all can change at the turn of your perspective.

Have you ever asked yourself, "What is the point of all this?
Why should I gain wisdom and be a good person or achieve goals
or attain wealth or try to bring justice to the world? I won't really
make a dent in social justice; how in the world will little ol' me
ever change the world? I never get picked anyway. What is the
meaning of life?"

You wouldn't be the first person to ask these questions. King
Solomon, one of the wisest men in history, had this dilemma and
wrote the Book of Ecclesiastes about his search to understand the
meaning of life.

He was searching for meaning, but he kept finding everything to be meaningless. King Solomon tried *everything*. He
tried the carefree life of enjoying wine and being lazy. He tried
a hardworking life, which led to success and wealth. When he

became king, he asked God for one thing: wisdom. God was so pleased by His request that He granted unprecedented wisdom to him. In the anointed wisdom Solomon experienced during his quest to find meaning, he concluded that nothing mattered. The more wisdom and knowledge he gained, the more grief and sorrow he realized.

You see, no matter how much we gain or experience, it will never be enough. It will all fade away. In the quest to fulfill our life's purpose and goals, it's easy to be plagued with anxiety from hustling, or a lack of joy. How is it that we aren't fulfilled even after reaching that big goal, or buying the new car, or losing the weight, or getting the cosmetic procedure? It never seems to be enough.

Recently, I was preparing to speak at a three-day conference. My hope was to change lives and to point as many hearts as I could to Jesus. I felt this pressure and tension in my chest. Do you ever feel pressure when you're walking in your purpose? Like you aren't doing enough, or you wonder if you are adequate? Do you get caught up in the logistics and practicalities and lose sight of the reason you signed up for it to begin with? That's how I felt.

Then one morning, I read the entire Book of Ecclesiastes. It was like the words were leaping off the pages, full of life and relevance this time. After all of Solomon's searching, he finally concluded that "there is nothing better than to enjoy and find happiness in our work because this is a gift from God" (Ecclesiastes 2:24).

Boom. Wow. Hello. So good. Yes.

Our purpose isn't supposed to make us feel burdened. Our short time on earth is a gift from God, and the best thing we can do is *enjoy* our calling. After I read this, I closed my eyes and imagined enjoying the conference, enjoying speaking to the

wide-eyed youth, enjoying preparing the talks with my husband.
As I did this, the pressure and tension began to melt away. I *de-cided* to have fun that weekend. God blew our minds and magic
happened!

The best way we can stay light and content is to enjoy the
process of using our gifts for God.

When you enjoy something, it doesn't matter if people notice
or not. It doesn't matter where you are in the process. If you
enjoy something, the outcome can't make or break you. When
you learn to enjoy, you can be in joy in almost every situation.

> *When you learn to enjoy, you can
> be in joy in almost every situation.*

Scripture says eternity has been placed in the human heart. That's
why we always feel this desire for more. Or maybe you've experienced a tension of contentment and longing. We *are* made for
more. The spirit within us was made for eternity. This longing
for more can deceive us into chasing meaningless things. Even
Solomon discovered and stated in Ecclesiastes 4:4, "Most people
are motivated to success because they envy their neighbors, but
this too is meaningless—like chasing the wind." But when we
enjoy where God has us, we get to relish in the gift of Kingdom
living, which is that *more* we crave.

Why are you working for success? Are you enjoying it? Why?

Nothing is certain in life. It is meaningless to work just to
build our own wealth, security, and success. If you aren't creating
with people you love and enjoy what you are creating, you will
miss the gift that God is handing you.

Many of us have the mind-set that we *have* to go to our jobs, study for a test, or show up on time. But truthfully, we don't *have* to do anything. When you get down to it, no one is forcing you. You are the only one responsible for the life you are creating. You may not be able to change your circumstances right now, but you can vastly change how you experience them. When you begin thinking *I get to* instead of *I have to*, your life will change. When you're saying things like, "I get to go to work; I get to go to work out; I get to cook a meal; I get to pay taxes; I get to visit my family," then you are suddenly back in charge of your life with a powerful perspective shift.

I used to have such an *I have to* perspective in some areas of my life. On days that my agent called to tell me I had an audition in one hour, I'd grumble to my husband "Ugh. I have to stop what I'm doing now and rush to make it to this audition." As if someone were twisting my arm. Think about it. No one really cares if you quit or don't show up. We may need to do certain things we don't like to do sometimes, but ultimately, we have the power to decide whether or not we do it. Then we decide the attitude we have about. The attitude of a powerful person or the attitude of a victim. Which will you choose? Once I decided to have a powerful attitude, it changed the way I approach last-minute auditions or low-rate booking offers. This is my process:

1. Do I want to do this?
2. Can I stay in peace if I say yes to it?
3. Can I enjoy it even in the hustle or unideal circumstance?
4. Will it be worth my time?
5. If the answer is YES to those questions, I choose to commit with an attitude of gratitude and enjoyment. If my answers are NO, I choose to honor my no. I graciously, yet directly, decline.

No one cares about the stress you endure when you commit to things out of pressure. The best thing is to remember you have the power to say *yes* and enjoy the commitment or to say *no* and keep your peace. Nothing is worth compromising your peace.

If you aren't living in alignment with your purpose, take a small step toward doing something about it. Insert your purpose and passion in your daily activities. Don't keep complaining about your situation. You are not a victim. Take responsibility for your current situation and do something about it. We can't expect anyone to help us if we don't help ourselves.

When it comes to walking in your purpose, keep these four thoughts in mind as your operating framework:

1. Cut out the things in your life that are draining you.
2. Enjoy the process of co-creating with God.
3. Enjoy expanding the Kingdom of God.
4. Love God and love people.

Cheers to a bright and free life of enjoying the gifts, calling, and destiny we have been given!

Enjoying Your life = The Sparkle Effect

Prayer

Dear Father:

I realize I have been striving so much for perfection. I want to make You proud, I want to show a return on the gifts You have given me, so I have been hustling through serving and checking goals off my list to make sure I am productive. I realize that You didn't mean for me to operate in survival mode or to focus on how big I can grow my platform.

You meant to give me a life in full abundance so I could love

You and love others from a place of rest and joy. Father, will You help me to have good balance in my life so I don't fall into the trap of laziness and unfruitfulness or into the sprint of achieving goals motivated by my own insecurity or envy? Lord, thank You for giving me the good health to enjoy eating, drinking, and doing my work.

I pray that I will maintain the good boundaries that will help ensure I am living the fullest life and able to fully partake in Kingdom living. Thank You for making life so much simpler than I thought. I will enjoy pursuing my dreams and loving people so that others will look upward because Your light shines so bright. Amen.

Wonder Words

"What do people get in life for all their hard work and anxiety?" It's all meaningless.

—Ecclesiastes 2:22

God has made everything beautiful for its own time. He has placed eternity in the human heart. We won't necessarily always see the whole scope of God's work from beginning to end so there is nothing better than to be happy and enjoy ourselves as long as we can.

—Ecclesiastes 3:11–12

So I saw there is nothing better for people than to be happy in their work. That is our lot in life. No one can bring us back to see what happens after we die.

—Ecclesiastes 3:22

It is a good thing to receive wealth from the Lord and the health to enjoy it. To enjoy your work and to accept your lot in life, this is indeed a gift from God. God keeps such people so busy enjoying life that they take no time to brood over the past.

—Ecclesiastes 5:19–20

chapter 23

Sparkle with Your Reputation

Her courage was her crown and she wore it like
a queen.

—*Atticus*

AS I entered into the prime age for peer pressure, I remember
my beautiful and popular friend, Jessie, inviting me to a party.
She was also the new girl at school and enjoyed a more welcoming
entrance than me. Everyone loved her—boys and girls. She had
clear skin and long, flowing blond hair and the coolest clothes.
For some reason, she liked me and actually invited me to a party.

I was scared to even ask my mama if I could go. Since I was
ten, she had me on a strike system that she used every time I
asked to go somewhere. I always got in trouble for being sassy or
talking back, so I got a strike every time I was sassy to her or even
rolled my eyes. If I got three strikes within a week, I was out and
couldn't do anything with friends on the weekend. Sometimes I
didn't even have to talk and I'd get a strike! It was a losing game
every time. It became useless asking to go anywhere.

For some reason, this time was different. Maybe my mama felt
sorry for me because I was in that terribly uncomfortable, inse-

cure, un-cute phase of puberty. For whatever reason, she not only said *yes* when I asked her to go to the party, she also helped me pick out my outfit.

I remember a few hours before I was supposed to leave, I was pitching a fit and freaking out that I didn't have anything to wear. Of course, my mom reminded me how fortunate I was to have clothes at all and what a selfish statement that was to make.

I wanted the boys to think I was hot and the girls to think I was cool. I didn't have anything remotely hot or cool in my wardrobe. Everything felt so uncool. *It still feels like this today come to think of it. I just don't mind anymore.* Our family didn't shop at name-brand stores.

I was up in my room pitching a tantrum, screaming that I didn't want to go anymore, raging about how ugly and stupid I was, while imagining scenarios of rejection. My worry came down to this question: "What if they don't like me?"

Do you ever ask yourself this question?

The fear of not being liked or accepted can drive us to do dangerous things. It will make us do things we don't even like and say *yes* when we really want to say *no*. The fear of not being liked will also make you a shell of a person. When we are so worried about fitting in, we try to become who we think we should be rather than radiating our true self.

My mama gave me a piece of advice that night as I was distressing and doubting my likability. She said to me, "Kristen, it is better for people to respect you than to like you." The wisdom in her words struck me, even in my immaturity. Not only did it feel true, it felt liberating.

Isn't it exhausting hoping to be liked? Do you feel like it magnifies all the ways you are insufficient or don't measure up? Do you place more value on others than yourself?

That night, I ended up wearing a white V-neck vest trimmed

in faux fur with silver metallic. Looking back, I wouldn't have let myself walk out the door like that. But at the time, I liked it because it sparkled.

I walked into that party hoping to be liked, but remembering what my mama had said. I was offered a mixed drink and kindly said "no." To my relief, no one questioned me. It took a lot of pressure off not trying to make people like me. I also realized that when you are confident in your decisions and the way you carry yourself, people respect that.

I stayed a few hours at this teenage house party. I didn't go to another house party again until after college. Going to more parties definitely would have made my social life at school better. But I realized that going to those parties wouldn't have been staying true to the essence of me. I simply didn't enjoy them. It's totally okay if you do enjoy them, by the way. I'm introverted, so I just prefer quiet. The point is to not compromise the way you act, talk, or think to get people to like you. Do what is true for you and own it.

Although it wasn't fun in the moment to choose respect over likability, my mama was probably right that it was worth it in the long run. Just like you, I always knew deep down it was a good idea to listen to my mama.

As an adult, the kind of clothes I wear or going to parties isn't my issue anymore when it comes to being accepted or liked. But I have struggled with overextending myself, showing up at everyone's event for fear that I will lose likability among friends if I say "no." What price do you feel like you are paying to be liked?

Please understand, there is nothing wrong with being likable. It's when you pay a price and compromise who you are to gain it.

The desire to be liked and accepted is a basic human desire. But when we desire pleasing people more than we desire pleasing God, it's a slippery slope that ends in compromise, indecisiveness, and a lack of knowing and honoring your true feelings. You may be thinking, "How do I get the bravery to say *no*? I don't want to lose my friends." Or maybe you have already set a standard in your relationships and don't know how to make that change without getting some resistance.

First of all, you have the spirit of power—not timidity or fear—living within you (1 Timothy 1:7). Pray and ask the Lord to embolden you with the power of the Spirit and then *just do it* even while you are still afraid. Doing something in the face of fear is courage.

Second, you don't have to worry about whether you'll meet resistance from friends and loved ones, because likely you will. Making changes for your good isn't always easy. It's just like working out. The soreness after working out hurts at first, but then your muscles get stronger and the fat around them melts away. You better keep truckin' and keep your eyes on the prize. You can do it. You are not a leaky love cup that needs to be filled. You are full and overflowing with God's love.

Let's look at the story of Joseph in the Bible. He had a great calling to be a leader, a man with great wisdom who could interpret dreams that would impact an entire nation. His brothers were jealous of him and took him out to kill him. But the oldest brother convinced them to sell him into slavery instead. The Lord was with Joseph and gave him favor and success in all he did. Potiphar was an Egyptian and captain of the guards who bought Joseph from the Ishmaelites, and Joseph became a slave in his house. When Potiphar saw that God was with Joseph, he made him in charge of everything in the house and entrusted all into his care.

Potiphar's wife noticed how handsome Joseph was and tried seducing him every day. She said to him, "Come to bed with me!" But Joseph did the right thing by God and refused to lie with her or be with her.

If the constant taunting and temptation weren't enough, Joseph met an even stronger resistance in doing the right thing. One day, there was no one else in the house and Potiphar's wife grabbed his cloak and said, "Come to bed with me!" But Joseph left his cloak with her and ran. In her embarrassment and frustration, she kept his cloak and told her husband that Joseph had tried to lie with her. She said after she screamed for help, he left his cloak beside her and ran out of the house.

Although there was nothing bad to say about him, she lied and accused him because she was offended. Potiphar believed her story and confined Joseph to prison. But even in prison, God was with him and gave him favor. The prison warden made Joseph in charge of all who were held there, and he was responsible for everything that happened there.

When we do what is right, we may still face opposition, false accusations, and even be found guilty. But not for long. When we do what is right in God's eyes, He is our vindicator and always restores what was stolen with a double portion.

Ultimately, Joseph is remembered for his ability to interpret dreams and is brought out of prison to interpret a dream for Pharaoh of Egypt. Before he even begins to interpret the dream, he says, "I cannot do this for you, but God can." Remember, Pharaoh of Egypt did not worship our God. He was an idol worshipper of many gods, so this was a bold and risky statement for Joseph to make, but he wasn't afraid. Talk about abandoning the need to be liked in order to do the right thing.

Joseph interprets the dream that none of the other wise men in the land could. He finds favor in Pharaoh's sight and is put in charge of everything in the palace and the entire land of Egypt.

Talk about restoration with a double portion. There were so many times it would have been easy for Joseph to grow weary in doing good. Why would he care about taking care of the prisoners or being kind to them? What would he gain from that? No one would recognize him or notice. But God was watching and saw Joseph's steadfast character even in the darkest, loneliest pit. He didn't compromise even then. He didn't compromise with Potiphar's wife, and he didn't fail to give God the credit before Pharaoh, who could have had him killed for his faith.

It's obvious that God honors those who honor Him. You cannot be a double-minded person, trying to be likable while also maintaining a Godly reputation. It's one or the other. One leads to life and the other leads to lifelessness.

> *You cannot be a double-minded person, trying to be likable while also maintaining a Godly reputation.*

You have the same God that Joseph did. Joseph isn't more special than you are. He believed in the dream God showed him for his life and made hard decisions that cost him likability among his brothers and Potiphar. They didn't have his best interest anyways. God elevated him to unlikely, unimaginable places. When you aren't worried about being likable, God can position you in unlikely places.

At the end of the day, no one could say a bad word about Joseph that wasn't true. You may face false accusations that you can't control, but God will certainly vindicate you. As long as you are upright in His sight, He will make His face to shine upon you.

Whose side would you rather be on? God's or those who don't

have your best interest at heart? Is there anyone for whom you are dulling your true self down?

If you want to start living an empowered life, reflect on the following:

- What have I been giving away that I don't want to?
- When do I say YES when I want to say NO?
- Whom do I have trouble saying NO to?
- What do I really want?
- What is the worst thing that could happen if I start saying NO?
- Do I trust God with the results enough when I say NO even when I am afraid?
- Why is it better to be respected than liked?
- How am I going to start developing self-respect?
- Why am I strong enough to start setting boundaries and standards?
- Who does God say I am?

You were made to be confident and secure—a bold woman who loves God, yourself, and others well.

Doing what it takes to be liked often requires compromising your radiance. You may be the only light anyone ever experiences, even that guy who needs to be reminded to honor your boundaries. Choose respectability over likability every time. That wisdom will preserve your reputation and never fail you in the long run.

Preserving Your Reputation = The Sparkle Effect

Prayer

Dear Father:

I am thankful that I can trust You when I make decisions that aren't easy or popular. In order to have the strength to start living differently I need to believe I am worthy and that You have wonderful plans for my future.

People may be confused or give me a hard time when I start making changes, and I am scared about that. Will You be by my side every step of the way so I can have the bravery and persistence to do it? God, it is more important to me to reveal the love and wonder of Jesus and Your love to others than it is to compromise my worth or reputation for the sake of being liked. Being liked now might feel better, but being respected lasts much longer.

Help me to see and feel the reward in doing the right thing now when it could mean losing a relationship. Help me to see that all I need is Your love. When I live for You, the right people will come into my life and the wrong people will go. I trust You, God. Amen.

Wonder Words

A good name is to be chosen rather than great riches, and favor is better than silver or gold.

—Proverbs 22:1

For the Lord knows the way of the righteous, but the way of the wicked will perish.

—Psalm 1:6

Only let your manner of life be worthy of the gospel of Christ, so that whether I come and see you or am absent, I may hear of you that you are standing firm in one spirit, with one mind striving side by side for the faith of the gospel.

—Philippians 1:27

chapter 24

Sparkle with Godly Boundaries

I don't care what they're going to say
Let the storm rage on
The cold never bothered me anyway

—*Elsa, from Frozen*

Do you ever feel confused by the difference between *loving* and *enabling?* If loving is so good, why do we feel violated or taken advantage of when we continue to help a difficult friend or loved one? We beat ourselves up for being selfish, but at the same time feel annoyed by the friend calling us for help yet again; we believe that we should sacrifice our time and say "yes" to everything and everyone who needs us.

Being compliant on the outside while feeling torn on the inside creates resentment in our heart. A lack of boundaries depletes our joy, and counterintuitively, strains our relationship with God.

I never kept boundaries with a friend I loved dearly. We grew up together since we were babies. I'd get so excited when she and her family came to visit that I physically got sick. Yes, that kind of sick...there were just so many butterflies! As I grew a little older, I started noticing she was never excited to see me. As a matter of fact, she would completely ignore me for the first few hours at family gatherings. I would wait for her to give me attention, which was usually something like, "Kristen, come in my room." I'd eagerly jump up, thrilled that she wanted to play or talk.

This kind of treatment continued for years, even into high school. I never understood it. How could I love someone so much who seemed to not care about me? She looked at me like I was beneath her. But the Bible says to "turn the other cheek," so I continued to be kind. I spoke to her first, let her borrow my clothes, and was always readily available to be with her, hoping things would change one day. One summer, she came to my family's house and brought her friends with her. For some reason they didn't have a car and wanted to go to the beach every day. She asked if she could drive my car. Even though I had to work, I agreed, hoping this would gain her love. She and her friends went to dinners and trips to the beach using my car and my family's beach chairs and towels, and they never one time invited me. One holiday I mustered up the courage to tell her how I felt.

I said, "I have always admired you and wanted to be close to you. You are so mature and I feel like you haven't wanted to be close to me."

She laughed. That was it, nothing else. She just laughed.

We ended up going to the same college. We were only two dorms down from each other, and when we met up, she was actually friendly to me. It was as if the heavens were lighting up the sky. There was hope! *I always knew she would come around.*

We both decided to join a sorority. She asked if she could borrow dresses from me. I was flattered she even liked my clothes because I always felt she was so stylish. So I let her borrow my dresses. We chose different sororities, which was no big deal I thought.

One day, I was walking through campus and saw her in front

of me. I called out her name. She turned around and I excitedly waved and said, "Hey!" She didn't say a word, turned back around, and kept walking with her new sorority sisters. I asked, "Is this how it's going to be?" She shot back, "I guess so."

When I got married, I invited her to my wedding. All I got was an RSVP, "No"; with no explanation, no kind note, not even a congratulations. When she got married, I wasn't invited. This was the final moment that showed me she truly wasn't interested in having a relationship.

Jesus did not come to make us doormats. He came so that we might have a life overflowing with the power of the Holy Spirit, and so that we might emulate the nature of Jesus. For the longest time, I lived under the common misconception that loving our enemies means taking abuse.

> *Setting boundaries is important because it trains people how to treat you and protects you so you can healthily love others.*

Studying how Jesus handled daily situations is the best way to learn how to truly behave like a Christian (Christ imitator). Jesus had great boundaries. Setting boundaries is important because it trains people how to treat you and protects you so you can healthily love others.

In *Boundaries*, Christian psychologist Dr. Henry Cloud compares us to a residential property. If a home doesn't have fences or doors, people can trample on your grass, ride their bikes through your flowers, and let their animals wreak havoc in your yard.

Neighbors can let themselves in unexpectedly. Without bound-aries, anyone can stay in your house, drive your car, and use your belongings without acknowledging you.

How does this analogy play out in your life right now? Does it feel like you're being walked all over? Maybe your feelings aren't considered by those with whom you are in relationships, or maybe they seem to be, but in a manipulative way. Do you feel like you have to say "yes" to everything? Do you feel guilty for saying "no"? Do you feel afraid that saying *no* will result in con-frontation?

You aren't made to feel guilty for saying *no* or resentful for say-ing *yes*. Knowing what God says about boundaries will help you live more powerfully and keep your sparkle.

Here are four biblical truths to help you set Godly boundaries in your life. (And pick up the book *Boundaries* by Dr. Henry Cloud and John Townsend to learn more.)

1. Control your property.

Galatians 5:22–23 tells us that "the fruit of the Spirit is love, joy, peace, patience, kindness, goodness, faithfulness, gentleness, and *self-control*. Against such things there is no law" (NIV). A pleaser is usually someone who is compliant on the outside, but who may feel resentful on the inside because they do not practice the spirit of *self*-control. I used to think self-control pertained to holding back from partaking in something pleasurable in the moment that isn't good for you. Like having that fifth slice of pizza or go-ing a little further with that guy than you originally planned. Then I learned something more life changing about the spirit of self-control.

Notice the word is *self-control*, not others-control. Learning how this plays out for you can give you a lot of freedom.

Here is an example:

A friend asks if she can come over and do laundry at my house. On one hand, I want to be a good person and share what I have with her. On the other hand, my current life is overwhelming and I have a lot on my plate. Do I stuff down my needs and let her come over so I look kind and generous? Or do I honor what I need and tell her it won't work out this time? I decide to try out boundaries and tell her it won't work out, but maybe another time. My friend gets upset and reacts with a passive aggressive remark. This is where self-control versus others-control comes in. I realize I can't control her reaction or how it made her feel. Her reaction is in her "yard." I am only in control of my yard, so I will not waver or beg for forgiveness or feel guilty for my decision.

Just like God doesn't force anyone to accept His answers, you can't force anyone to like yours either. But, you *can* control *your* decisions, responses, and reactions. As the sole protector of your heart, you not only have the right, but you have the responsibility to steward what is allowed inside, whether it be people or feelings. With Godly boundaries, you can be totally okay when someone doesn't like your decision. Learning to be okay when someone is mad at you for being true to you is a mark of freedom and confidence.

2. Guard your heart.

Although Jesus said that we should operate as a unified community as the body of Christ, there are separate homes and properties in a community. Properties have fences with gates to let the good in and keep the bad out. It is important to guard our well-being from intruders or clingers, but equally important to receive goodness, help, and love by letting it all in or out through opening the gate. You may need to evaluate what or who is currently on your property. It could be people who are bringing you distress and confusion. Or it could be feelings of weakness, guilt, and bitterness. It's time to let the bad out to make room for some good to come in.

Jesus says, "Do not give dogs what is sacred; do not throw your pearls to pigs. If you do, they may trample them under their feet, and turn and tear you to pieces" (Matthew 7:6 NIV). You are sacred. Your heart is sacred. You don't have to keep giving it to someone who tramples on it and tears you apart. If you are currently in a situation like this and want to keep this person in your life, it's time to have a conversation to let them know your relationship dynamic needs to change. Otherwise, be like Princess Elsa and sing the *Let It Go* song.

3. Know the difference between a boulder and a load.

This is my favorite concept Dr. Cloud explains in his book, *Boundaries*. "Carry each other's burdens," says Galatians 6:2, "and in this way you will fulfill the law of Christ" (NIV). This verse shows our responsibility to one another. Verse 5 goes on to say that "each one should carry his own load." The Greek words for *burden* and *load* give us insight into setting Godly boundaries.

The Greek word for *burden* means "excess burden," or burdens so heavy that they weigh us down. This is when we are responsible to helping someone carry weight they cannot carry on their own. The Greek word for *load* means "cargo" or "burden of daily toil." These are the daily responsibilities that need to be carried out in order to function in life.

In this Scripture, Jesus is calling us to help people do what they cannot do for themselves, because that is what He did for us. We are each responsible, however, for doing what we are capable of doing.

For instance, if you know someone who is constantly asking for a ride somewhere simply because they don't like to drive, that would be categorized as a backpack load. A backpack load is light enough you can carry it on your own. A friend who is grieving the death of a family member is dealing with a boulder, or excessive load. Excess load is when it reaches beyond our capacity to carry it on our own. This is when you step in to be the hands and feet of Jesus for them. In your daily life, practice discerning which kind of loads your friends are carrying. If a friend continually forgets her homework and wants to copy you, that would be a backpack load. You don't need to feel the pressure or responsibility to let her copy you. However, if you do have a friend asking for help with a backpack load and you *want* to help her with no pressure attached, that's completely fine. As long as you don't feel resentful. As the body of Christ we are called to share in each other's burdens, not enable irresponsibility or laziness.

4. Check your motives.

The Bible says to do everything as if we are working for God, not people. If you are driven to do something out of any motive other than love and to bring glory to God...first, do a heart check to see if you can reset. If not, don't do it at all. Many of us know when we are being taken advantage of, even by the sweetest, most well-meaning people. Yet we continue to drive ourselves crazy, dropping everything in order to come to their aid. Why do we do this? Some of us fear that if we stop helping, we will no longer be needed, or we will cause conflict, or we will be discarded.

In the Gospel of Matthew, Jesus tells His followers, "Whatever town or village you enter, search there for some worthy person and stay at their house until you leave. As you enter the home, give it your greeting. If the home is deserving, let your peace rest on it; if it is not, let your peace return to you. If anyone will not welcome you or listen to your words, leave that home or town and shake the dust off your feet" (10:11–14 NIV). Jesus doesn't tell His followers to stay and take abuse.

Setting boundaries is not being mean; it's actually loving. You cannot effectively love yourself and others if you do not sustain your mental, emotional, and spiritual health. Be prepared that some people will not adapt to your new boundaries, which is fine. If someone leaves you because of this, it was not a healthy relationship in the first place and you need to let the "bad" out to make room for the good to come in. And take heart, it could eventually come back around.

Now that I have learned about setting Godly boundaries, I don't repeatedly open my heart to someone who isn't interested in receiving it. I no longer feel the need to pursue a relationship with someone I love who doesn't love or respect me. In summary, be a young woman who is open to conversation if someone is willing to change. Remember that "NO" is a complete sentence. Until then, remove yourself from relationships that only hurt you so you can draw nearer to God and love people with a whole heart.

Godly Boundaries = The Sparkle Effect

Prayer

Dear Father:

Thank You for loving me so much that You don't require me to be physically abused or mistreated. I understand that "turning the other cheek" is a humble posture of the heart. Lord, will You show

*me where I am allowing unhealthy things into my heart space? I
want to be strong and to stand firm in guarding my heart. I want
to believe I am worthy of setting boundaries. Help me to be like Jesus in the way He was able to love His enemies without being a
doormat. Thank You for being my shield and defender. In Jesus'
name, Amen.*

Wonder Words

---

*Make no friendship with a man given to anger, nor go
with a wrathful man.*

—Proverbs 22:24

*Do not be unequally yoked with unbelievers. For what
partnership has righteousness with lawlessness? Or what
fellowship has light with darkness?*

—2 Corinthians 6:14

*The LORD is my chosen portion and my cup; you hold
my lot. The lines have fallen for me in pleasant places;
indeed, I have a beautiful inheritance.*

—Psalm 16:5

*It is better to live in a desert land than with a quarrel-
some and fretful woman.*

—Proverbs 21:19

*As for a person who stirs up division, after warning him
once and then twice, have nothing more to do with him.*

—Titus 3:10

chapter 25

Sparkle with Positive Relationships

The challenge that so many people have is not
knowing how to take that first step of reaching
out to another person for help.

—*Kate Middleton*

You cannot accomplish great things alone or while in unproductive relationships. You need a team around you who will
bring out the best in you. You need to be in relationships with people who believe in you and who will help you manifest your dreams.

> *You need to be in relationships
> with people who believe in you and
> who will help you manifest your
> dreams.*

It is absolutely amazing how quickly a positive, light-filled person can be darkened when they enter into a relationship with a

person who is negative. We think we are invincible, that surely we will raise them up to see the light, too. Even if there is one negative person in your core group, it won't take long for them to affect the dynamic. The old saying is true, "It only takes one rotten apple to spoil the whole bunch."

That doesn't mean you should be unkind to anyone. You don't have to gossip about someone else in order to protect your positive relationships. But it is important to protect your inner core with vigilance because those relationships help enhance your sparkle.

Deciding who to let into your inner circle requires discernment and wisdom. Something to consider when making this decision is your personality type. For instance, on the Strengths-Finder personality test, one of my strengths is being a relator. A relator is someone who prefers to go deep and spend quality time with the people she feels closest with. She holds those important relationships with sacred regard. For example, as a relator preparing for Miss USA, I enjoyed working with a small team of people who really cared about me. Because I like to build deep and trusting connections, it worked best for me to surround myself with people I knew were for me. I encourage you to take the StrengthsFinder test, which you can do online and learn about how you operate in your strengths. It will help you create thriving spaces for the best way you relate to others. The people you surround yourself with have a voice in your life, so it's important to filter who gets that kind of access and influence on your mind.

Motivational speaker Jim Rohn notably said, "You become the average of the five people you spend the most time with." That is how small your inner core can be. Whether you are preparing for a pageant or another goal, you are a leader as God's daughter, even if you don't see yourself as one yet. A queen has a court to help advise her through her reign. You have a call on your life and you need to surround yourself with a court, too.

Ask yourself these questions:

Who are the closest people surrounding you right now?

Do you admire their qualities?

Are they people you want to be like?

Are they full of Godly wisdom?

Do you trust they have your best interest at heart instead of their own self-interest?

You may not have an inner circle yet; maybe you have some developing to do.

Here is how to decide who your core should be:

1. Family

Family members like a sibling or parent can be awesome to have in your inner circle because you can be honest and open with them. They will have your back and love you unconditionally. You can usually let your hair down and say things with family members you can't say around other people. Your family knows your heart and will speak candidly with you when you need it. My mother and sisters are definitely on my inner core list. Sometimes it can be hard to hear truth and criticism from family because we want them to be proud of us! Constructive feedback is almost always rooted in love, even when harsh. We need truth speakers in our life who will keep us grounded. It's the private places where we are refined that help us face public trials.

2. Mentors

Our peers may not always be the best inner core members because they can be susceptible to fall into traps of jealousy and comparison. Choosing a mentor who is older than you, some-one you admire and who has accomplished, or has helped others accomplish, similar goals is incredibly valuable to have in your corner. Look for someone who is very secure in who they are and won't compete with you, even subtly. It's important to look at the fruit of someone's life and notice how they talk about others. Do they keep information confidential? What is their relationship like with others, and do they reveal information about their other mentees? If so, be very discerning in what you share with them, or look for a different, more reliable mentor. A mentor could be a family member, a teacher, a pastor, a life coach, or someone you look up to who has achieved success in your goal space.

3. Boyfriend/husband

If you have a supportive boyfriend or husband, he could make a wonderful inner core member. It can strengthen your relation-ship to confide in and help each other. Men and women think and process differently, so it will help balance your mind having ac-cess to a man's perspective in dealing with conflict or in decision making. When I moved to Los Angeles, I was in a long-distance relationship. My boyfriend at the time was very involved in help-ing and did everything he could to make the transition easier for me. He was a great source of encouragement and advice, even from afar. My husband, Kris, is my closest confidante now. He is constantly motivating me, editing my writings, and praying with me. He is my sounding board and offers guidance on how to handle situations with Godly wisdom. It is imperative that your romantic relationship be supportive. Can you talk to him about anything? Does he listen to you intently and give thoughtful, ob-jective feedback? If so, great. If not, consider his strengths, how you can depend on him, and in what areas you need to depend on someone else.

4. Best friend

I said before that peers may not be the best inner core members because of the jealousy or ego that often arises. But a close friend who isn't in your space and doesn't have an interest to be in it in the future can be a very helpful inner core member. She or he can be great comic relief and remind you not to take yourself too seriously. In high school, I had a friend named Liz who was an awesome friend in my inner core. She excelled in the violin and I loved musical theater. She was smart and driven but didn't share an interest in things like running for class president. We had different personality types and she helped balance out my intensity with her good humor. We went to each other's performances and strongly supported each other. Is there someone in your friend group like that? If so, it may be wise to spend more time with her and invest in that relationship.

A great inner core best friend will most likely have different strengths and skill sets than you, which is important and nourishing for your growth. For example, I am a visionary, so details like spreadsheets and logistics are not my strength. I have these grand ideas, but the thought of executing them can often overwhelm me. I have two friends in my life I often call on to help me talk through a plan of action. Who is there for you when you need help in an area in which you don't thrive?

5. Coach

Hiring someone to teach and coach you can really take your training or personal growth to another level. Just make sure they keep all information from your time together private. One strong benefit of a life or pageant coach is their objective perspective. They will see you as *you* without the context of your daily life. You may also feel a different kind of openness to share emotions, thoughts, and matters of the heart with someone who isn't so intertwined in your life. Coaches can move you from point A to point B faster than trying to figure it out on your own. I offer coaching through my blog, SheIsMore.com, and would love to work with you!

Now that we have addressed the different kinds of people to consider for your inner core, these are the five types you need around you:

1. The encourager

You want someone who will pray with you, intercede on your behalf, and remind you of the God qualities in you. You should feel rejuvenated after talking with them.

2. The truth-teller

You need to balance out encouragement with accountability and honesty. This should be someone from which you receive constructive criticism well and who truly cares for you. You will never grow unless you can be honest with yourself, and sometimes it takes another set of eyes to call out our blind spots.

3. The wise one

You need someone you can run ideas or dilemmas by. You trust them to be your sounding board because they have a deep, fruit-bearing connection with God and offer unbiased advice. The way they live their life will be evidence of their wisdom.

4. The expert

An expert in your field of aspiration will help you think outside the box, present ideas, and push you to aim higher. They will be able to give you inside information because they have been there and done that.

5. The strategist

You absolutely need an organizer, someone who is detail oriented and knows how to connect the dots of your vision. They are the one who puts a plan of action into place to help you go from the idea phase to the implement phase.

You may have read these lists and thought, "I don't have anyone like that." Maybe you feel really lonely and excluded right now. My word for you is this: Whatever you resist persists. If you believe no one wants to surround you, you will put off that vibe and reap that self-fulfilling prophecy. Your vibe attracts your tribe. Change your beliefs about how you relate to other people. Be bold and start reaching out to people to build positive relationships. I know it can seem scary at first, but remember you are a queen. All you have to do is step into the radiance of your true identity because it's already within you.

Building Positive Relationships = The Sparkle Effect

Prayer

Dear Father:

Please help me to determine who I need to surround myself with. Help me realize that You created relationships and that I am made for connection. I often want to do everything on my own because I don't know whom I can trust. Lord, I know You say bad company ruins morals, and I want to live a life worthy of my calling. Please help me to see who I need to let go of and give me the grace to do it kindly and respectfully. Strengthen me to stand firm in my decision and to not allow the reaction of a friend or family member to cause me to crumble. I want to know what it feels like to understand that developing an inner core and protecting it is not self-centered; it is wise. I know that when I walk with the wise, I will become wise, too. I no longer want to be brought down or allow others to stifle my potential. I pray that You will divinely appoint exactly who I need in my life and that we will recognize and vibe with each other right away. In Jesus' name, Amen.

Wonder Words

Above all, keep loving one another earnestly, since love covers a multitude of sins. Show hospitality to one another without grumbling. As each has received a gift, use it to serve one another, as good stewards of God's varied grace.

—1 Peter 4:8–10

Whoever walks with the wise becomes wise, but the companion of fools will suffer harm.

—Proverbs 13:20

A man of many companions may come to ruin, but there is a friend who sticks closer than a brother.

—Proverbs 18:24

Iron sharpens iron, just as one man sharpens another.

—Proverbs 27:17

Do not be deceived: "Bad company ruins good morals."

—1 Corinthians 15:33

chapter 26

Sparkle with Forgiveness

When you are happy you can forgive a great
deal.

–Princess Diana

On the road to your dreams, you will face heartbreak of many
kinds. Girl-to-girl pain is some of the hardest to endure. I believe friendship breakups can be worse than romantic boy-girl
breakups. We were created for relationship with other women,
but the enemy knows the power in that. Satan causes division
in hopes of turning friends into frenemies. Even older women
are susceptible to being intimidated by younger women. Maybe
you have been treated unusually unkindly by an older woman.
You couldn't understand it because it just didn't make sense. You
didn't do anything wrong.

We see this same sentiment played out in *Cinderella*. Why
is the stepmother so heartless and demeaning to Ella? She does
everything she is supposed to do and more. She never talks back
or questions her stepmother's unkindness. Finally, the stepmother
crosses the line. She confronts Ella with the glass slipper she
found in Ella's secret hiding place in the attic. When the step-

mother realizes Ella could have a chance at marrying the prince, she breaks the slipper to pieces, shattering the only hope Ella had in years. At last, Ella asks the question we've been wanting her to ask the whole movie, "Why? Why are you so cruel?" The stepmother replies: "Because you are young and innocent and good. And I..." She doesn't finish the sentence. She doesn't need to. We can draw our own conclusions based on our own experiences.

Have you ever felt like Ella, confused about why you are the victim of harsh verbal, physical, or psychological treatment? Their mistreatment isn't because you are bad. It's because they are hurt. Maybe you have been in the stepmother's shoes. Maybe you have endured pain and grief and it hardened you. In whichever shoes you may be, hurt people hurt people. Many times the teachers, leaders, or family members who should be protecting us, offering love and comfort, don't have the capacity to give it.

On the one hand, it's a good thing to let this kind of adversity motivate you to rise above it. As a matter of fact, our enemies can propel us upward. On the other hand, be careful—it isn't healthy to be motivated by spitefulness or bitterness. That's when we end up hurting others rather than helping. You don't want to end up like the stepmother.

How do you know when you're using your pain to motivate you in a healthy way? First, if your intentions to rise are good, you have likely forgiven your enemy. You have allowed your trial to give you compassion for others rather than a need for revenge.

Your heart is like a garden. Keep your heart tender by watering it with your tears. Allow yourself to feel pain and cry out to God for comfort. Fruit and flowers can't grow in the desert. Cacti do, but they are prickly. Don't allow your heart to go through a drought by numbing yourself out. Tears last for a night, but shouts of joy come in the morning. Those who sow in tears will reap with songs of joy! Tears have the power to keep your heart pure and strong.

Tears last for a season—and that's the growing season. Use your tears to your advantage. This is a growing, mending, healing, and pruning season. While your circumstances are looking less than ideal on the outside, consider what God wants to water within you.

One of the many things the Lord is continually watering within me is the ability to forgive. Forgiveness is so important because it's a weapon we must sharpen and use many times throughout our life. Unforgiveness, however, harbors hardness and bitterness in our heart's soil. It squelches the growth of beauty and fruit.

Jesus warned about the folly of unforgiveness as He told the parable in Matthew 18:31–35 about an unforgiving man who had been forgiven a great debt by the king:

Then the king called in the man he had forgiven and said, "You evil servant! I forgave you that tremendous debt because you pleaded with me. Shouldn't you have mercy on your fellow servant, just as I had mercy on you?" Then the angry king sent the man to prison to be tortured until he had paid his entire debt.

"That's what my heavenly Father will do to you if you refuse to forgive your brothers and sisters from your heart." (NLT)

Having unforgiveness in our hearts is like sentencing ourselves to torture in our own prison. Forgiveness is powerful. It sets us free to continue to love. We can't sparkle if we are holding on to grudges.

You are made for more. You are made to be secure in who you are so you can fully forgive others.

> *You are made to be secure in who you are so you can fully forgive others.*

Here are four things to consider that will make forgiveness a little easier:

1. Spiritual warfare

It's important to understand you have an enemy that works many angles to distract and disrupt you from the abundant life Jesus died to give you. The enemy uses people to tear you down.

The Bible tells us that our struggle is not between flesh and blood, but against the spiritual forces of evil in the heavenly realms (Ephesians 6:12). I have experienced this firsthand. Once, some close friends made accusations against me, attacking my character. I was distraught and couldn't sleep the night it happened. The next morning, I was on a plane to Orlando for work. I was red-eyed and anxiety-ridden from a sleepless night of tossing and turning. *Why would they say such things? Why would they want to believe these things? Why would they want to hurt me?*

I decided to use the flight as undistracted time to process it with God. I closed my eyes and asked Him those questions and began to journal what I heard Him speaking to me. He reminded me who the real battle was against. He showed me a picture of the enemy using my friends unknowingly to distract me from the good things unfolding in my life. It made sense; I recalled the look in their eyes as they accused me. It was vacant and unrecognizable. Has someone ever accused you of something? Usually, our immediate reaction is to defend ourselves. But defensiveness fuels the fire. What should you do instead? Pray and ask the Lord to give you eyes to see into the heart of the matter. The person hurting you is likely hurt inside. When God shows you their hurt, it gives you the compassion to let your guard down and the humility to validate their feelings. They don't have to be right in order for you to validate how they *feel*. When a person feels seen and heard, it can change the course of conflict. Humility begets humility. If you can avoid your need to win, you will diffuse the conflict faster, thus killing the enemy's power.

Use your mouth to speak over the situation! "Devil, you will NOT cause division between me and my friend! I WILL forgive her and I won't let you use her against me! Be gone, Satan!"

Jesus said, "Father, forgive them for they do not know what they are doing" (Luke 23:24 NIV).

Jesus knows that people are often blind to themselves. I've heard it said that the people cheering "Hosanna!" for Him on Palm Sunday were the same ones shouting "Crucify him!" days later. People, even our close friends, can turn on us. Like Jesus, we must remember they are being used and do not know what they are doing.

Whether or not you acknowledge it, you are in the midst of a spiritual war with the enemy. Satan is the father of lies. He comes to steal, kill, and destroy. That is exactly what he was doing through my friends that night...and what he has even done through me at times. Unfortunately, we can all be susceptible to the devil using us to hurt others. That's why it's important to stand guard against his tactics because he prowls around like a lion, looking for someone to devour. When you understand spiritual warfare, you'll be enabled to show mercy to your accusers and cling to God, who is your refuge in the face of attacks.

2. Remember.

When someone offends me, I sometimes catch myself in a thought like one of these:

"I am shocked such a close friend would instigate division."

"I can't believe she would talk to me like that. I would never treat someone that way."

"Did he seriously just un-invite us to that event? Who does that?"

When we are wronged by someone else, we act like we would never do such a terrible thing. But we have. We just forget because it's much easier to be the victim than to be responsible.

God showed me something else on that flight to Orlando. He flashed in front of me the last several times I had hurt someone. None of them were outright. Because I'm not a mean girl...right? They were mostly undercover jabs hidden in a compliment about someone. One of those passive aggressive ways to get a point across, while still appearing nice. It broke my heart. Suddenly, I thought, *Who am I to be shocked by how someone else acts? I am no better.* It would be even worse if all my thoughts turned into words and were broadcast for people to hear. Can you imagine that? Just look at the people in the news lately who have had their private e-mails, in-person conversations, and text messages exposed to the public. Would any of us be innocent if our private thoughts and conversations were exposed? Next time you are offended, remember at least the last five things for which God has covered you.

When I do this, I am quickly humbled to see that the sins of my inner person far outweigh the offense I am upset about. When I remember how much God covers my dark moments, it immediately becomes an honor and joy to forgive my offender.

> For if you forgive other people when they sin against you,
> your heavenly Father will also forgive you.—Matthew 6:14
> (NIV)

I don't know about you, but I don't want my unforgiveness to block God's forgiveness of me. Don't be discouraged if you still feel negatively triggered by someone who hurt you after forgiving them. Most of the time, we have to forgive someone more than once. It can often be an ongoing process. I know that I have needed forgiveness more than once. Even Jesus' disciple, Peter, was perplexed about how many times someone could be forgiven. When he asked Jesus about it, His response was "seven times seventy."

I have literally experienced a withholding of blessing in my life because of unforgiveness. I noticed I wasn't booking any print jobs or commercials I was auditioning for. I didn't book for nine months, which is the longest time I have ever gone without booking. I prayed my heart out, updated my portfolios, got callbacks, and kept a positive mind-set. I would get so close, but the booking would go to someone else. What in the world was going on? I prayed to God for understanding and heard a soft voice in my head, "You are harboring a grudge." I knew exactly who He was talking about. It took weeks of pride swallowing, but I let go of that grudge with the help of a lot of prayer.

Here's the thing. Forgiveness doesn't make the other person right. True forgiveness frees you of the toxic power an offense or person has on you. Sometimes we can get to forgiveness without having a direct conversation with the person who hurt us. But often, it requires a conversation. It requires us to see that person and the situation through God's eyes. It requires a breakthrough. If there is someone who has a hold on you now, it's time to move on. The enemy is the one winning. It's time to face this person or this pain head on and tackle it. You have a destiny to fulfill and you won't be able to do it in the fullness of God's blessing when there is unforgiveness.

3. Do right in God's sight.

Forgiveness doesn't necessarily mean reconciliation, which can be very sad. Our primary motivation for forgiving someone can't be reconciliation. It simply must be our obedience to God in full trust and surrender so we can be like Him. Reuniting is wonderful and can definitely happen, but what matters most is that you are in upright standing with God and you have freedom in your heart.

Whether or not someone repents and receives your forgiveness is not your concern; it's God's. We just need to emulate Christ by forgiving someone for unknowingly allowing the enemy to work through them, and then surrender the results to God.

4. Pray and bless.

God has a higher justice system than ours. How can we conquer evil with evil? We can only really conquer evil with good, which is why God calls us to deal with our offenders in a way that can make our guts wrench to think of it. Not only does He want us to forgive our enemies, He wants us to pray for them *and* bless them. Say what? I don't know about you, but my flesh screams, "Ah—no! Why?"

I used to struggle with this a lot. The last thing I wanted to do is pray for someone who offended me. But one day as I was reading through the Gospel of Mark, I had a revelation. It said, "You have heard that it was said, 'Love your neighbor and hate your enemy.' But I tell you, love your enemies and pray for those who persecute you, that you may be children of your Father in heaven...Be perfect, therefore, as your heavenly Father is perfect" (Mark 5:43, 48 niv).

He calls us to love and pray for our enemies so that we may be His children...so that we may be perfect like our Father. That is all I need to know. All I care about is being like Christ. Because I know if I do that, He'll take care of things I can't control. This might sound out of touch with reality and overly spiritual, but I have truly experienced that the more Christlike decisions I make that grate against my natural reaction, the more beautiful I become within. He'll do the same for you.

In the awaited moment when Ella walks out of the house with the prince, her stepmother comes down the stairs. Ella turns around to face her intently and says, "I forgive you." I know, how'd she do that so quick? She just smashed her glass slipper and called her a wretch!

The reason is because Ella was wise. She knew that if she was going to reign with compassion instead of hardness, she had to leave the poison behind. She wasn't saying, "I'm okay with what you did and you can come live in the palace with me." She was saying, "I'm not taking you with me."

Forgiveness says, "I'm done with the power you had over me." Will you be brave and water your heart with tears? Will you let pain soften you toward compassion instead of harden you with bitterness? Ask yourself, "Who or what poison do I need to leave behind? Who do I need to bless when I really want to curse?"

Love conquers all and makes it possible to forgive. Love is your greatest weapon against evil, so don't let unforgiveness steal your most powerful tool. How will you steward your pain in order to reign?

Forgiveness = The Sparkle Effect

Prayer

Dear Father:

You know the pain I feel. You see the pain inflicted on me. Thank You that not one small detail in my life goes unnoticed by You. Thank You for being my defender and fighting on my behalf, even when I can't see. Please help me to relinquish my need to control people and situations by talking about the person or the problem. Please strengthen me with the power of the Holy Spirit to put a watch guard over my mouth and to stay silent amid accusations and gossip. It's so hard to feel helpless and defenseless. I want to fight for myself. I know when I try to defend myself, I'm not trusting You to do a much more powerful work in redeeming me than I can. God, please help me to feel the freedom that comes from praying for my enemies. I want to be a mature daughter, but I can't do it in my own flesh. I need the empowerment of the Spirit to defy my natural tendencies and to actually bless those who curse me. I declare that flesh begets flesh, and spirit begets spirit (John 3:6). Thank You for being true to Your Words and promises. In Jesus' name, Amen.

Wonder Words

If your enemy is hungry, give him bread to eat, and if he is thirsty, give him water to drink.   —Proverbs 25:21

And whenever you stand praying, forgive, if you have anything against anyone, so that your Father also who is in heaven may forgive you your trespasses.

—Mark 11:25

Then Peter came up and said to him, "Lord, how often will my brother sin against me, and I forgive him? As many as seven times?" Jesus said to him, "I do not say to you seven times, but seven times seventy."

—Matthew 18:21–22 (NLT)

But I say to you who hear, Love your enemies, do good to those who hate you.

—Luke 6:27

Be kind to one another, tenderhearted, forgiving one another, as God in Christ forgave you.

—Ephesians 4:32

chapter 27

Sparkle with Self-Discipline

*If you do your best each and every day, good
things are surely to come your way.*

—*Tiana, from The Princess and the Frog*

Life is a race and the key to winning is how we run it. We see this displayed in the classic tale in Aesop's fable of "The Tortoise and the Hare." You may recall that the tortoise, a very slow animal, and the hare, a very fast jackrabbit, are running a race. The hare starts out running fast and is confident he will win, so he stops to take a nap. While he is napping, the tortoise keeps moving along slowly and ultimately wins. The moral of the story is that slow and steady wins the race. Not only that, but the quiet humility of the tortoise kept him focused on his task, whereas the pride of the hare was his downfall.

A goal or a dream can seem so far off and so many years away. When we look at those around us who are light-years ahead in progress, we wonder, "Why am I even trying to make a mark in the world? Other people are already doing it. I am not needed."

But that mentality is a problem. When we are focused on the result, the promotion, or the title, and not the journey, then we *will* fail. We may actually reach the goal, but we certainly will not be happy once we get there because the way we journeyed was wrong.

When God spoke to my heart about being a communicator of His Word all over the world in 2012, I started preparing. Little by little, I learned and grew. The closer I grew in relationship with God, I became convicted of things I needed to change. I said "no" to certain kinds of modeling and commercial jobs. This was hard as it was my main source of income and I didn't want to lose favor with my agents. Although no one may notice or care if I did a lingerie job or a seductive, hamburger-eating commercial, I made the decision not to.

By God's grace, I've experienced exponential growth, but also stagnant and dry seasons. During those times I began studying all the women leaders and ministers. I read their bios, did their Bible studies, listened to their podcasts, read their books, went to their conferences, and even got to interview some of them on my TV show. I observe qualities these women emulate that I need to cultivate. Do you have role models you look up to like this?

Sometimes I feel on top of it, and sometimes I feel so behind. The thing is, we never really "arrive." No matter how many books I write, conferences I speak at, followers I have on Instagram, views I have on YouTube, resources I create, women God allows me to reach, there will always be more ground to cover. It's that feeling that says, "there must be more." Do you ever yearn for more? I believe we experience the tension of wanting more when we have enough because eternity is placed in our hearts. There *is* always more. We will realize the fullness of it in Heaven one day. Until then, God always wants to cover more ground and He wants to partner with us to do it. That's why it's better to go at the race slow, steady, wise, and ready.

Here are five ways to have the self-discipline to run your race well:

1. When God gives you a vision, do it.

One of my greatest strengths can also be a big weakness. On the StrengthsFinder test I mentioned previously, another of my top five strengths revealed is that I'm an *activator*. This means when I have a vision or a great idea, I get super excited and want to make it happen *now*. I make quick decisions and get to work on them immediately. But when the project starts to drag out, I lose steam or feel discouraged and then quit for a period of time. I put activities off when I think it will take too long to see results.

As I've grown spiritually and in self-awareness, I am able to notice when I'm losing steam. As you are working on your dream or goal, recognize that there is a force resisting your efforts. It could be one of your strengths playing out as a weakness. It is super important to know your strengths, weaknesses, and patterns so you can use them to your advantage. The enemy doesn't want you to fulfill God ideas, so he attempts to destroy them by defeating you. Recognize that onset feeling of defeat or discouragement and snap out of it. Take your thoughts captive, don't let them captivate you. It's better to be proactively positioned against a downward spiral than reactively digging yourself out of it.

Remember that moment God gave you the dream and how it made you feel. It might have been five or even twenty years ago, but the dream is still relevant because it hasn't been brought to its fullest fruition. He gave it to you and it was real and you can pick it back up at any time because the Lord is on your side.

2. Pretend that you already are who you want to be, then live like it.

Imagine you are already exactly where God has called you to be in life, in that dream career or position. If that's hard to do, imagine a person you admire who does something like what you want to do. What does their day look like? What time do they wake up? Do they exercise, eat healthy food, take vitamins? Are they social? Do they take time for themselves? Are they on the road a lot with a hectic schedule? How do they treat their enemies? How do they treat their followers? You may answer these questions and realize you actually don't want that life at all.

But if you do, then get to work and start to model your life to emulate the life of your dreams. Be intentional about this every single day. It's the self-discipline and consistency in everyday life where real change happens. Be the change now in order for change to come.

> *It's in being self-disciplined and consistent in everyday life that real change happens.*

3. Become who you want to be.

Not only is it wise to consistently do the things that will prepare you for that promotion or career goal, it is also important to notice the character qualities your dream requires. Character and integrity equal longevity. Taking shortcuts, going behind backs, and manipulating your way up the ladder may get you the promotion earlier, but you may lose respect and burn bridges along the way. Maintaining integrity means taking a loss or being overlooked sometimes, but God always upholds the righteous. We may not be getting fast promotions, but we are certainly getting spiritual promotions, which ultimately prevail.

Who is someone in your field of interest you admire? For example, Christine Caine and Lysa TerKeurst are two of mine, so I look to them to see what their personal qualities are. They are honest, hardworking, transparent, generous, passionate, opinionated, strong, and humble, and they love God with all their heart.

Whom do you admire and what qualities of character do they possess?

4. Focus on what you do privately and consistently.

What we do in our private life furthers or hinders the realization of our dream. Keep your eyes focused on your work and chip away day by day, even when you feel hidden or unseen. There may be some days you don't know what to do, or maybe you can't afford the resources it would take to make something happen. In those moments, you can whip out your journal and strategize with God. You can brainstorm, make lists, and research. You can also cry sometimes when you feel overwhelmed and defeated. Be gentle with yourself through the ups and downs.

Sometimes I avoid social media for weeks because I have to protect my mind from getting defeated by everyone else's progress. It's the only way I can stay focused on the daily work it takes to accomplish a big project. It may sound extreme, but sometimes you have to take extreme measures to cultivate self-discipline and eliminate distraction.

We can get a lot more done when we stay focused on producing an idea rather than talking or posting about it. In 2016, I launched and led my first women's retreat called The Daughter Gathering. It had been on my heart for a while. I was nervous and afraid, but when I finally decided to go for it, God completely and supernaturally covered it. Many people didn't even know I did it until after it was completed. I didn't post or talk about it publicly in the process because I needed to stay focused on planning and preparing. As a society, we are addicted to affirmation. But reaching your dream isn't just about what people see; it's about how you manage your time on a daily basis.

5. Remember that what you do now leads to promotion later.

Don't wait to get the title, the promotion, or the relationships to start doing the work that comes with them. Don't wait to become Miss USA to start doing charity work or being aware of your Instagram posts. Don't wait to get the dream boyfriend in order to stop settling for less. Don't wait to be booked on a job in order to start acting. We have so many tools at our fingertips now to create our own outlets to do what we love or want to do. There really is no excuse for why we can't be doing what we love.

Our job is to start doing what God has put on our hearts little by little, day by day, in the midst of unknown and wobbly steps of faith. Then trust that promotion will come when we are prepared. The race has to be about the journey, the growth, and the relationships you form along the way. The race is ultimately about becoming who you are meant to be, then the *doing* will fall into place.

Remember: Slow, steady, *and disciplined* wins the race.

Self-Discipline = The Sparkle Effect

Prayer

Dear Father:

Please give me the endurance and patience I need to focus on producing good works in my life, even when I don't see results. Lord, I want my life to honor You. I want to live a life worthy of my calling.

God, help me to eliminate distractions and pridefulness. Help me to see the moment I am about to start fading and losing hope so I can reset my mind on You and pray for strength. I never want to come into the dangerous agreement with the enemy that leads to self-pity and defeat.

God, I pray for a fresh revival of my dream and a new burning to take place in my heart. Infuse me with enthusiasm, and the self-discipline to sow the seeds of my purpose each day. Give me clear vision and renewed hope in You so I can feel Your energy flowing through me in everything I do. In Jesus' name, Amen.

Wonder Words

Work with enthusiasm, as though you were working for the Lord rather than for people.

—Ephesians 6:7

We ask God to give you complete knowledge of his will and to give you spiritual wisdom and understanding. Then the way you live will always honor and please the Lord, and your lives will produce every kind of good fruit. All the while, you will grow as you learn to know God better and better.

—Colossians 1:9–10

We also pray that you will be strengthened with all his glorious power so you will have all the endurance and patience you need. May you be filled with joy, always thanking the Father. He has enabled you to share in the inheritance that belongs to his people, who live in the light.

—Colossians 1:11–12

chapter 28

Sparkle with Influence

Behaving like a princess is work. It's not just
about looking beautiful or wearing a crown. It's
more about how you are inside.

—*Julie Andrews*

You are an influencer. The question is, how are you stewarding your influence? People are watching you even when you don't
think they are (1 Corinthians 8:9).

You are God's princess. You are royalty. When you embrace
your role as a daughter in God's Kingdom, you immediately become an influencer. You are an ambassador of Christ and His
marvelous Kingdom of beauty, light, truth, and reconciliation.

> *You are an ambassador of Christ*
> *and His marvelous Kingdom of*
> *beauty, light, truth, and*
> *reconciliation.*

His princess is always aware that she could be impacting someone's life. She holds herself to high standards in the way she dresses, speaks, and behaves for the sake of her own honor and for the sake of younger girls seeking a role model.

God is an identity changer. He changed the name of Jacob (deceiver) to Israel (may God prevail). He changed the name Abram (high father) to Abraham (father of multitude of nations). When you accept Christ, He changes your name, too. Christian means "Christ follower" and Christ means "the chosen one; the anointed one." You are chosen and transformed into a Christ imitator. You may be the only example of Christ a person will ever see. When people encounter you, do they experience a glimpse of Jesus? Experiencing Jesus through you will look different than it does through someone else, so don't compare yourself. I used to think I needed to be soft spoken and quiet. God gave you your personality so He could shine through you uniquely. For instance, I'm very passionate about the truth and what is right versus wrong. I express this through the sassy personality God gave me. I encourage you to sit down and reflect on the personality traits God gave you. You may even believe them to be bad. That might be a good place to start. I used to think my opinionated sassiness was bad because it made me strike out on my mom's discipline system as a teenager. Sometimes the devil can use our unbridled strengths to our detriment, when they were really intended to be used for God's glory.

The way you live your life should not be taken lightly. Jesus knew exactly how and when you would receive His invitation to become your Prince and how it would transform your life. Now it's time to be an example in your daily life of what living in the radiance of your true identity looks like.

You have influence, and the way you steward it matters. The Bible says we are ambassadors of Light; God is making His appeal through us. We speak for Christ when we live as if we believe God is good.

As ambassadors for the Kingdom, we have the great responsibility and honor of being the light of the world. We have influence in any realm we are in, whether we are stay-at-home mothers, students, entrepreneurs, work in ministry or in the corporate world. You may think you aren't making an important impact, but someone is always watching you whether you know it or not. Even the way we manage our social media can change lives, negatively or positively.

Here are things to consider for stewarding your influence well:

1. Post with virtuous intent.

A picture is worth a thousand words. What messages do your photos send your followers? Do they honor you and other women? Are they in alignment with your royal identity? I'm not sure that mine have always been. Modeling is one of my professions, so I used to share swimwear and lingerie photos. But the closer I drew to God, I felt a stirring in my heart not to share these photos. Before that, I received a few anonymous messages on my website condemning modeling photos, calling me a hypocrite or asking how I defined modesty. Those messages only made me defiant. No message or correction you receive from others will spark a true heart change. It was only when I drew nearer to God and experienced His gentleness that I wanted to change. Real, meaningful change happens in the heart through relationship and intimacy with God. This is why I don't have a hard rule for what not to post when it comes to modesty. My decisions come from my relationship with God. Yours can, too. As you draw nearer to Him, just check in with the Spirit before you put up a post. You can ask questions like, "Why this photo? Whose attention am I trying to attract? Why do I want their attention? What can they give me that God can't?" When I asked myself some of those questions, I went on a deleting binge.

The more intimate in relationship you are with Him, the clearer you will be able to discern how to practically steward your influence through the photos you post.

If you find yourself debating whether or not to share a photo, it's good to err on the side of caution. If you don't have peace about it, don't click "post."

2. Post positive status updates.

The messages you post on social media could literally be a letter to your followers about the heart of God in your life. Sadly, Christians generally get a bad rap. As you probably know, many people are turned off or have been damaged by believers. Thankfully, you can change that for someone. It's crucial for the sake of others that we manage our influence with diligence. Don't get overwhelmed and take on the weight of the world. Remove any pressure that might be coming over you right now. All you can do is plant seeds. God will make them grow.

Some people may never read the Bible but will watch you on social media. What kind of language do you use? Is it wholesome and uplifting? Do you use social media as a place to vent or to talk about a meaningful matter or how God is working in your life? How do you respond to a rude comment on your page?

We are not perfect, but we certainly don't need to take to our keyboard every time we want to vent about something. Use your social media platform for purpose. I'm not saying to create a facade and paint a glossy, perfect picture, because illusions don't help anyone. A great guiding principle for posting on social media is a balance of real life mixed with hope. It's important for people to see that you struggle, but *how* you struggle is what sets you apart—by turning to prayer, community, and faith.

3. Protect yourself in your weak moments.

Sometimes we have to be real and let our hair down. But it isn't wise to do that with anyone and everyone. You need a select group of people you can trust to cover you in weak moments. Think back to the list of inner core members you made in Chapter 25. Keep a tight, close-knit circle around you who understands they aren't seeing the entire version of you in your moments of venting or shortcomings. Not everyone needs to know when you drank too much and blurted out things you would never say soberly. Don't fuel a gossip firestorm. There are "friends" in your life who may have an interest in exposing you or using it against you later. Do not let your guard down around them. Ask the Lord to sharpen your discernment so you can be cautious in what you share.

4. Be moderate in public.

Be aware of how much you drink and how you behave in social settings. With Snapchat, Instastory, and our ability to upload a picture or video "in the moment," our actions are not restricted to a party or place anymore. Have fun without too much alcohol, or without any at all, and that behavior is good stewardship of your influence. Know your limit and stick to it.

Not overdoing it while out can also protect you from becoming a victim. To see a real-life example of someone who was tragically targeted, watch the documentary *Audrie & Daisy*. Audrie Pott was a high school student in Florida. She went to a party one night and drank so much she passed out. Some boys sexually molested her, drew all over her naked body, and took pictures on their phones. Not only did they text the photos out to fellow students until the entire school saw them, they were also posted online. Audrie was called names, abandoned by her friends, and bullied. Surely Audrie wouldn't have believed her peers were capable of such cruelties when she went to the party. And the results of these boys' abuse was too much for her to bear. She couldn't handle it and asked her mother to pick her up from school early one day. Later, when her mother went to her room to check on her, she found her daughter hanging from the shower, dead.

In today's insta-world, it takes only one time for someone to let their guard down to ruin their life. One click can damage a reputation or ruin the chances of a career goal or a dream. And it takes only one daughter of the King to step in and use her influence for the protection of others if she sees injustices underway.

Yet I believe many of us don't hold ourselves to a high standard because we believe we aren't that important. Maybe we aren't popular at school or anywhere for that matter. Believing you don't matter is when you stop living as the queen you are called to be. This is a follower mind-set. You don't have to be famous to have an impact. The truth is, you are called to be a leader. As His daughter, you are called to be the light of the world. God has transformed you from a pauper in the crowd to a princess with a crown.

Do you have the mind-set of a pauper or a princess? A princess knows she is accountable for her actions and she stewards her influence in high regard. It doesn't matter how big or small it is because those who are faithful with little will be trusted with much (Luke 16:10).

Are you carrying yourself like royalty? If not, what needs to change?

Royal Influence = The Sparkle Effect

Prayer

Dear Father:

Thank You for trusting me to be Your ambassador. I am sorry for thinking less of myself than exactly who I am. God, please wash me clean of small-mindedness and selfishness. Create in me a heart that cares about other people, and their relationship with You.

Father, You have changed my life; You are my rock and redeemer, so I never want to cause anyone else to stumble as they are seeking You. When people encounter me, I want them to encounter the kindness of Jesus. Father, please open my eyes to be aware that in every situation I am impacting others.

Give me the discernment to know what to post and what not to post on my public profiles. I want to live a life worthy of my calling, so show people the hope of Heaven that is found in Jesus. Amen.

Wonder Words

May integrity and uprightness preserve me, for I wait for you.
—Psalm 25:21

She is clothed with strength and dignity.
—Proverbs 31:25

Blessed are those whose way is blameless, who walk in the law of the Lord! Blessed are those who keep his testimonies, who seek him with their whole heart, who also do no wrong, but walk in his ways!

—Psalm 119:1–3

You are the light of the world—like a city on a hilltop that cannot be hidden.

—Matthew 5:14

So let's stop condemning each other. Decide instead to live in such a way that you will not cause another believer to stumble and fall.

—Romans 14:13

chapter 29

Sparkle with Teachability

Even miracles take a little bit of time.

—*Fairy Godmother, from Cinderella*

You can't achieve your dreams by doing what you *think* you know. The moment you think you have all the knowledge and skills to achieve your goal is the moment you have lost. There is a difference between confidence and arrogance—while we should be selective about the advice we take and from whom we take it, we must maintain a posture of teachability in order to grow.

I wouldn't say I was ever the most talented in any activity I got involved in, but I was very hardworking. I joined the swim team when I was eight years old and had no clue what was going on. I joined the team late so I had missed about two weeks of practice. My first introduction to the swim team was *competing* in the first meet of the season. I remember thinking, *What is a swim meet? Like we meet and swim?* I got there and was thrust on the diving block, which I had never even seen before, amid the bustle of adults with whistles and timers around their neck. I remember a lady with blond hair yelling at me to dive in and swim to the end of the pool as fast as I could in "freestyle." *Umm what is freestyle?* I also didn't dive. I jumped.

There were other kids lined up in the lanes next to me ready with their goggles and swim caps. I didn't have either. My eyes were bulging out of my face in panic, but I didn't have time to think. At the shocking sound of the foghorn, I jumped in and flapped around in my version of freestyle in the water, while gasping for air with every stroke, my eyes wide.

Needless to say, I didn't win that event. I came in second-to-last and even my eight-year-old self decided this wasn't good enough. I worked my little determined tail off that whole summer. I watched how the older kids swam, noted their diving and turn techniques, and spent extra time with my coach outside of practice. Even at eight years old, I wanted to learn and be better and spend time with people better and older than me. At the end of the season, I received the Most Improved Award. I went on to compete on my high school varsity swim team for three years. I was never the fastest or the best, but I still got to compete in the "big leagues" and list the experience on my résumé for scholarship and college applications. The point is, I wasn't the best or most talented, but staying coachable paid off. It will pay off for you, too!

One of my best friends, Nia Sanchez, is one of the most coachable people I know. It's actually one of her biggest strengths. I met Nia when I was making an appearance as Miss USA at the Miss California USA pageant. She was competing for the first time. I remember sitting in the audience and feeling completely drawn to her. She wore an ice blue gown and radiated from the inside out. She was my pick to win and I remember thinking to myself, *That girl is going to be Miss USA one day.*

She placed 2nd runner up! But she wasn't finished yet. After I moved out to Los Angeles, we became friends. She competed again and placed in the top 20. Then a third time with a top 20 finish again. You see, although she radiated, it didn't guarantee her a win quite yet.

In 2014, she decided to give her shot at Miss USA one last chance by competing at Miss Nevada USA. Over the years, she spent time with people she admired, grew more in her relationship with God, and became more confident. In her preparation for Miss Nevada USA, I was impressed that she sought out wisdom from me and our other friends who are former titleholders. She could have easily acted like she had it all together.

Many well-meaning people wanted to give Nia advice. She graciously accepted what people had to say, but discerned who to really listen to. She was highly coachable with people she knew had her best interest at heart, who had a proven track record of success, and whom she respected and admired. The night she walked out onstage at Miss Nevada USA, I knew it was hers. She sparkled.

Then, in her training for Miss USA, she remained coachable. She probably became even more coachable because the stakes were higher. As a matter of fact, several evenings she was at Miss USA, we skyped and drilled in mock interview. Nia not only listened to my feedback, she quickly *applied* it. She wasn't afraid to mess up in front of me because she knew it was better to do it with me in practice than with the judges on game day. Being coachable means you're willing to show your weakness in front of someone who may even feel intimidating. Nia wasn't afraid of what I would think because she knew making mistakes was a part of her *training for reigning*.

Nia's humility and wisdom in being coachable paid off. I remember sitting in the audience at Miss USA in Baton Rouge, Louisiana. She walked out onstage in her red evening gown and lit up the entire venue with her smile. She nailed her final questions with passion and certainty. When the top five did their final look, the craziest thing happened. I've never seen anything like it. The judges were captivated by her, taking photos of her in the top five. She was emanating so much sparkle and glow, it felt like fireworks going off in the place. I had never witnessed such a slam dunk win.

You can have a slam dunk win at your dream, too. Being coachable is one of the crucial components to having the Sparkle Effect.

I believe one of the biggest downfalls we can make on the road to our dream is when we are stubborn and hardheaded. Being strong-minded and staying true to who you are is absolutely necessary, but don't get the two confused. Pride goes before destruction, and an arrogant spirit before a fall (Proverbs 16:18).

Ruth is one of my favorite examples of a woman in the Bible with a teachable spirit. Not only did her willingness to listen impact her life greatly, but it made her an ancestress of King David and Jesus Christ. Her lineage most likely received a generational blessing of teachability because of her.

When Ruth's husband died, she was left a widow. She had no idea what her future looked like or how she'd be taken care of. It would have been ideal for her to remarry in that day. Instead, she pledged her devotion to her mother-in-law, Naomi, and her God instead of the pagan idols of Ruth's tribe, the Moabites. She made the noble decision to accompany Naomi to a new land out of love and loyalty. Ruth did her best in the new land and was determined to earn a living for herself and her mother-in-law, who was too old to work. She listened to the wise counsel of Naomi and went to work in the fields of Boaz, a wealthy and Godly man. Out of compassion, Boaz purposefully left extra grain for Ruth and commanded that she be untouched and protected.

When Naomi saw the favor Ruth had gained in the sight of

Boaz, she advised her again. One day Naomi said to Ruth, "My daughter, it's time that I found a permanent home for you, so that you will be provided for. Boaz is a close relative of ours, and he's been very kind by letting you gather grain with his young women. Tonight he will be winnowing barley at the threshing floor. Now do as I tell you—take a bath and put on perfume and dress in your nicest clothes. Then go to the threshing floor, but don't let Boaz see you until he has finished eating and drinking. Be sure to notice where he lies down; then go and uncover his feet and lie down there. He will tell you what to do."

"I will do everything you say," Ruth replied. So she went down to the threshing floor that night and followed the instructions of her mother-in-law (Ruth 3:3–6 NLT).

Ultimately, Boaz married Ruth, bought her mother-in-law's land, cared for Naomi, and they had their first son Obed who was the grandfather of King David.

Ruth was in the royal bloodline of the Messiah. God redeemed her misfortune by giving her favor with Boaz, whom she never would have met if she hadn't listened and followed the advice of Naomi.

I don't think it's any coincidence that her great-grandson, David, writes: "Listen to advice and accept discipline, and at the end you will be counted among the wise" (Proverbs 19:20 NIV). What you do now, the wisdom you accept and follow, not only affects your life, but your children's lives, the lives of their children, and the lives of generations to come.

No matter how much education or experience you have, a teachable heart will always give you a winning edge. "Whoever exalts himself will be humbled, and whoever humbles himself will be exalted" (Matthew 23:12 ESV).

> *No matter how much education or experience you have, a teachable heart will always give you a winning edge.*

Maybe you're in a position where you want to learn and grow, but you don't have anyone you can reach out to for guidance. I have been there, too. For many seasons and dreams in my life, I have turned to books for motivation and guidance. The other day, I made a list of all the dreams I had accomplished in the last few years. I realized that every single one of them was supported by a book I had read that gave me either an idea or that extra boost of confidence to take a leap of faith.

A person with humility listens to advice and never thinks she knows it all. Being teachable with an eagerness to learn and grow makes you sparkle.

In summary, here are some things to remember about coachability:

1. Don't quit at something you aren't great at yet. Keep working at it.

2. Be bold in asking for advice. People love to feel like they have something valuable to offer.

3. Choose the right people to coach you.

4. Don't be afraid to ask your role model for mentoring. Nia listed me has her role model on her Miss USA bio and it was an honor to offer gold nuggets to help propel her forward. It could be an honor for your role model to help you as well.

5. Be willing to mess up in front of your coach/mentor/parent during training. That's the best place to do it.

6. Listen to advice and then *apply* it.

Teachability = The Sparkle Effect

Prayer

Dear Father:

Thank You for loving me so much exactly where I am, and for loving me too much to leave me there. Thank You for being my transformer. Your Spirit lives within me and gives me the power to transform more and more into Your image every day. Like 2 Corinthians 3:18 tells us, "But we all, with unveiled face, beholding as in a mirror the glory of the Lord, are being transformed into the same image from glory to glory, just as by the Spirit of the Lord" (NKJV). Dear Lord, I pray You will give me the discernment to know whom to listen to and from whom I should accept advice. I pray You will send mentors into my life who will take the time to pour into me and speak the truth and instruction I need to grow into the woman You created me to be. Amen.

Wonder Words

Where there is no guidance, a people falls, but in an abundance of counselors there is safety.
—Proverbs 11:14

The way of a fool is right in his own eyes, but a wise man listens to advice. —Proverbs 12:15

Make your ear attentive to wisdom and incline your heart to understanding.

—Proverbs 2:2

Likewise, you who are younger, be subject to the elders. Clothe yourselves, all of you, with humility toward one another, for "God opposes the proud but gives grace to the humble."

—1 Peter 5:5

chapter 30

Sparkle with Boldness

Venture a little outside your comfort zone. The
rewards are worth it.

Rapunzel, from Tangled

One of the most valuable lessons I learned on my road to
the Sparkle Effect was how to be bold. Part of my prize package
as Miss North Carolina USA was a week-long leadership and
mental management intensive in Dallas, Texas. It was a program
called Eagle University, and it gave me a winning edge. While
attending the intensive, I listened to incredible speakers and did
eye-opening exercises that empowered my goal-setting. Plus, it
was great to connect with the other state titleholders who were
there as well.

The week was about much more than learning how to win
a pageant. It was about how to win in life—how to dream big
and see our dreams transform into reality. I took away one simple
phrase from that week that still impacts my life today: *The answer
is always "no" until you ask.*

When the instructor said this, a wave of clarity washed over
me. Any fear I had of asking for what I wanted or needed seemed

to physically dissipate. As I've said before, we can't accomplish our dream on our own. We need help and support from others. In my case, one of the things I wanted to accomplish was singing the National Anthem for a UNC vs. Duke basketball game. I needed to find the right person to open that door of opportunity. And that door wouldn't open without me knocking.

What door are you waiting to knock on?

Often, the only thing standing between where you are now and your goal is an ask. The possibility of a "yes" could bring you one step closer to your dream. After that week at Eagle U, I realized the worst thing that could happen in asking for what I needed is the answer "no." Why is "no" so scary? Maybe because you put yourself out there with the risk of getting rejected. But that only has to do with your ego. We have to get over ourselves to go beyond ourselves. In reality, man's rejection is God's protection and a "no" leaves you right where you were before. This means you have nothing to lose in asking, so what fear is there in rejection?

I remember coming back home from the conference feeling invigorated. I went to Staples and bought a business card holder to organize all the business cards I had received at my appearances so far. I made a list of all the things I needed to prepare for the two-week competition at Miss USA. Then, I looked through the business cards to see who I could ask for help.

I needed about twenty outfits for all the events, photo ops, and rehearsals at Miss USA. I also needed shoes, jewelry, makeup, personal training, skin care services, teeth whitening, luggage, hair products, and beauty tools. Thankfully, some important things like my competition gown were already sponsored.

My family and I didn't have the finances to buy everything I needed, so I had to learn the art and power of asking.

As Jesus said in the New Testament, "Ask, and it will be given to you" (Matthew 7:7 NIV). "Whatever you ask in my name, this I will do, that the Father may be glorified in the Son" (John 14:13 ESV).

It is biblical to ask for what we need. We can't hope someone will read our minds or wish on a star. We can't worry what people will think when we ask. I still make these mistakes. Studies have shown women have a harder time than men asking for what they want or need. As daughters of God, let's decide not to be a part of that statistic. We have been given a spirit of boldness, not timidity, so let's tap into it and be brave.

> *We have been given a spirit of boldness, not timidity, so let's tap into it and be brave.*

At an event, I interviewed Jennifer Garner for her movie *Miracles from Heaven*. On the red carpet, her publicist said there would be no time for us to take photos with her. When I had my one-on-one interview with her later in the press junket, I respected the publicist's boundaries and didn't ask to take a photo. I didn't want to appear aggressive or inappropriate. I felt a little jealous later when I saw several of the other journalists had been bold and gotten a photo with her.

Our natural reaction is to get mad at those who get something we were told we couldn't have. The difference between those people and us is they *asked* for what they wanted. Maybe you are an innate rule follower like me and don't like to ruffle feathers. I have never been rewarded or recognized for being a nice rule follower. I've actually felt overlooked because of it. Can you relate?

Even Jesus required the lame man and the blind man to ask for what they wanted. He wants us to want our desire enough to have the faith to ask for it.

By the time I got to Miss USA, I felt proud that almost everything I used to compete was entirely sponsored, loaned, or gifted. The process of asking, pitching, and negotiating with businesses certainly required a lot more work than simply buying whatever I wanted, but it taught me some valuable life skills. I learned to think like a businesswoman. I learned that businesses rarely give free handouts and they need to feel they are receiving something valuable in return. I developed relationships. I learned how to pitch a mutually beneficial ask to a company. The process of asking fostered in me grit and backbone.

In my interview at Miss USA, the judges specifically asked me about the cost of my interview dress and pageant wardrobe. In that moment, I excitedly expressed how it is possible to live your dreams even without having the financial means. Much of it is made possible by the power of asking.

Here are a few pointers to help you craft an ask:

1. Think from the perspective of the person you ask for help. If you were them, how would helping you be beneficial? What could you offer them? For instance, I asked a marketing expert to help me with a project *after* I offered to help him promote his workshops in LA.

2. Remember you are giving someone a chance to partner alongside your dream and to help you. If they say yes, don't fall into the trap of feeling indebted to them beyond what you agreed upon. For instance, I know a young woman who doesn't ask for help because she feels the person will hold it over her as leverage in the future. Don't let that fear stop you. Even if someone does try to hold a favor over you, that doesn't mean you have to play that game with them. A favor is a favor.

3. Be considerate, thoughtful, and direct in your approach.

4. Be sure it checks out in alignment with God's Word and will *before* you ask for something.

5. Explain the positive qualities you like about a company or person and why you specifically have chosen to reach out to them. Explain how their partnership would help you and how it would benefit them.

6. Make your ask in person or over the phone. It is much easier to turn someone down in a text or an e-mail.

What is on the other side of your ask? It can't leave you any worse than you are now. So you might as well ask. Even if you don't get a yes from someone, they may redirect you to someone who can help.

Before asking something of another, consider these questions:

- What are some things you need right now?
- Which ones can you take care of yourself?
- Which ones do you need help with?
- Who are some people you can ask?
- How can you honor them in asking?
- What value can you offer them in return?

Remember, Queen, you have God on your side. He is within you and you will not fail. Hold your head high and be bold, gorgeous. You have a mission to accomplish and you can't do it alone. Don't let timidity steal another day. The help you need could be one ask away.

Boldness = The Sparkle Effect

Prayer

Dear Father:

I don't like asking for handouts or being dependent upon anyone. It makes me feel like I will be trapped in owing people things. Will You help me break free of this stronghold? Help me to receive help as a gift, not as a loan with strings attached. God, will You please make clear to me what Your will is? I often think I need to know specifics for my life, but really, I just need to make sure the nature of my desire is in alignment with the nature of You. I want to delight more in You so my desires will start to match Your will more and more and shape my nature.

God, will You please help me to recognize where I need help and to know who would look favorably upon me, and would You give me the bravery to connect with them? I have often not brought my hopes and requests to You because I feel You are too busy and my problems are too small. Please show me how to be strong and to boldly present my requests at Your throne.

You created me to be relational and interdependent. I want my dream of _____ to come true and I can't do it alone. Amen.

Wonder Words

Ask, and it will be given to you; seek, and you will find; knock, and it will be opened to you.

—Matthew 7:7

Therefore I tell you, whatever you ask in prayer, believe that you have received it, and it will be yours.

—Mark 11:24

If you then, who are evil, know how to give good gifts to your children, how much more will the heavenly Father give the Holy Spirit to those who ask him!

—Luke 11:13

If you abide in me, and my words abide in you, ask whatever you wish, and it will be done for you.

—John 15:7

Do not be anxious about anything, but in everything by prayer and supplication with thanksgiving let your requests be made known to God.

—Philippians 4:6

You ask and do not receive, because you ask wrongly, to spend it on your passions.

—James 4:3

chapter 31

Sparkle with Peace

All it takes is faith, trust and a little bit of pixie dust.

—*Peter Pan*

Did you know you don't have to struggle with anxiety? It can be a thing of the past. One of the many things I love about being God's daughter is that I no longer have to let worry or anxiety take over. Worry is not a fruit of the Spirit, of God's nature, or a part of our inheritance. When Jesus was in His final days on earth, He said to his followers: "Peace I leave with you; my peace I give you. I do not give to you as the world gives. Do not let your hearts be troubled and do not be afraid" (John 14:27 NIV).

It's natural to process through how to deal with a bad situation. But the key to stopping anxiety before it starts is to focus on the solution, not the problem. I know that stress and anxiety can come on so strong, it feels impossible to control sometimes. What if peace came on so strong, it washed away every tension and fear? What if you started experiencing peace and calm as your immediate reaction to a stressful situation? You can. It's called soul training.

Soul training is training your soul to match the Spirit. When you give your life to Jesus, the Holy Spirit comes to live within you. You have your soul and the Spirit. One of the characteristics of the Spirit is peace. The key is to consciously and proactively choose peace, which defies your natural anxious response. The more you choose the Spirit of peace, the bigger it grows and the more it becomes etched into your soul as a natural reaction. It says in the Word that Jesus left peace for us. Isn't that so cool? He invites you to *continue* in the peace He left for you.

You may be thinking, *My circumstances are far less than peaceful, Kristen.* That may be true, and I totally get it because I've definitely been there. Jesus didn't make promises about changing our circumstances. He promised peace in the midst of our circumstances. This is much more powerful than needing external factors to be calm and settled in order to have peace. We get to *stay* in peace no matter what as long as we *choose* it.

There are so many things we can get caught up in or worry about. Worry is a result of not being able to control something. Honestly, it would make sense to worry if we were the only ones in control. But thankfully we aren't! We are in partnership with the God of the universe, and He is in control. Praise the Lord! He enables us to do our best, and God will do the rest. What a relief!

Many of us find our identity in doing, serving, and accomplishing. We are *yes* people and can feel resentful when we aren't appreciated, or we get overwhelmed with meeting too many commitments. Or maybe that's just me. There isn't anything wrong with doing and serving until all that busyness leads to worry and anxiety. Suddenly, we are so busy doing good things that we aren't connecting to God.

I love the story of Mary and Martha in the Bible and always reread it when I need to get centered again.

Now as they went on their way, Jesus entered a village. And a woman named Martha welcomed him into her house. And she had a sister called Mary, who sat at the Lord's feet and listened to his teaching. But Martha was distracted with much serving. And she went up to him and said, "Lord, do you not care that my sister has left me to serve alone? Tell her then to help me." But the Lord answered her, "Martha, Martha, you are anxious and troubled about many things, but one thing is necessary. Mary has chosen the good portion, which will not be taken away from her." (Luke 10:38–42 ESV)

Jesus spells it out. All we really need is Him. Everything else that causes us to worry is temporary and will ultimately be taken care of by Him. Joyce Meyer says worrying is like a rocking chair; you can rock all day but it won't get you anywhere.

I'm sure many of us can relate to Martha. We are busy caring for everyone and doing for others, which isn't wrong. But when we spend time with the One who cannot be taken from us, that is when we get fueled with the peace that transcends all understanding. In that relationship, we can cast our cares upon Him because He cares for us.

We have to stop filling our schedules with things that drain us and start spending time with the One who fulfills us.

In the Gospel of John, it describes when Jesus meets the woman at the well. He asks her for a drink and she shuns him for asking her because she is a Samaritan and he is a Jew. It says:

Jesus answered her, "If you knew the gift of God, and who it is that is saying to you, 'Give me a drink,' you would have asked him, and he would have given you living water." The woman said to him, "Sir, you have nothing to draw water with, and the well is deep. Where do you get that living water? Are you greater than our father Jacob? He gave us the well and drank from it himself, as did his sons and his livestock." Jesus said to her, "Everyone who drinks of this water will be thirsty again, but whoever drinks of the water that I will give him will never be thirsty again. The water that I will give him will become in him a spring of water welling up to eternal life." The woman said to him, "Sir, give me this water, so that I will not be thirsty or have to come here to draw water." (4:4–15 ESV)

In this story, the woman realizes she needs a different kind of water to fulfill her than the one she's been drinking. She needs the deep refreshment that comes from Holy Spirit. He quenches the thirst of our hearts and souls when we are rung out and exhausted. When I am in a flow of spending quality time with Jesus, I am more peaceful and joyful in the midst of expectations and chaos. He fills me, and my cup runneth over. I can calmly do things that usually make me anxious, like host or plan events.

I have not always enjoyed hosting gatherings in my home. I used to get nervous and worried that guests would be uncomfortable or that they might judge its lack of style, simpleness, and my lack of homemaking talents. When Kris and I got married, this was a bit of an issue because he could care less what our house looks like before he invites people in. Our house could be a hot mess with Kris's protein shake–encrusted bottles and leftover chicken plates strewn in unlikely places across the house. Yet he'd invite friends to come home from the gym with him. I'd be startled when they strolled in, me in a sports bra and dirty dishes in the sink. I'd either hide in a scurry or start feverishly washing dishes. In an effort to appear as the hospitable wife, I'd nervously offer his friends a drink. All the while hoping they'd say "no," because our dishwasher leaves spots on our glasses!

Do you feel a lot of pressure to seem like you have it all together? That pressure will make us anxious and ultimately unhappy. The pressure we put on ourselves pushes out His peace.

I also like to be on a schedule and know where I'm going and when. When the rest of the world isn't quite on my schedule, it throws me off kilter. I suddenly find myself gripping for control I don't have, which grips a tightness in my chest.

Giving in to worry and anxiety enslaves us. Staying in the peace of Christ starts in our mind. If we aren't proactive about keeping our inner peace in check each day, it will be easy to let reactive emotions take over.

Every morning, I set three intentions for the day in my journal. One intention I always set is to stay in the peace of Christ, which channels everything through the peace filter that day. Whether you are taking an important exam, having a breakup conversation, going to a party, waiting for a result, or getting unexpected news, there is a peace power living in you that can help.

When I first started speaking, my entire body would get racked with anxiety. I felt unqualified. *What if I don't sound confident and smart? People will see that I am an impostor who shouldn't be onstage.* I almost called one event organizer and backed out.

But then I realized that would completely go against what I wanted to speak on . . . confidence in our royal identity. So I had to talk back to my anxiety. I had to cast my cares on God. He was the One calling me to speak, so He was going to have to qualify me. All I had to do was be obedient, enjoy the process, and trust Him to follow through. And He did, of course. When does He not? Only when we take the control back and push in our own strength. The good news is we don't have to be strong. The Bible says it's in our weakness and reliance on Him that we are made strong. Where God guides, He provides.

It's time you start talking back to your anxiety and stressors, too! My friend Christa said it beautifully, "You are the priestess of your temple, the queen of your soul." Take your authority back and tell those stressors who is boss. If God has called you to do something, you get to do it in peace and joy. You don't have to worry about letting Him or anyone down. Look at all the great heroes of faith He called in the Bible. Moses had a stuttering problem, yet God used Him to save the people of Egypt. Sarah was past her childbearing years, yet God enabled her to give birth to Isaac. Noah was an ordinary guy who lived righteously and had radical faith in the midst of public ridicule. If God calls you to something, He will bring you through it, so you might as well save yourself anxiety and do it in peace.

It's not your circumstances making you worry; it's how you think about them. Focus on God and how much bigger He is than your seemingly big problem. Your mountain is His miracle. We are created to do the possible, and God is in charge of the impossible.

You can be in the middle of uncertainty and still keep your peace because you know God is certain about His good waiting for you on the other side.

Let go of what and who you can't control and let God be God.

Sounds easy enough. But fully letting go is hard. We may want to trust God, but for some reason, there is a block. Does thinking of God as a Father throw you off? Sometimes we can project qualities of our earthly father onto our Heavenly Father. Maybe your dad was aloof or checked out when you needed him. Maybe he was hard on you and never told you what you needed to hear. The truth is even the best father figure can let us down. Our earthly fathers were never designed to meet all our needs. If they were, we wouldn't need God. God loves you uniquely the way you need to be loved. He is not aloof or checked out. He isn't distant or far away. He isn't a tyrant impossible to please. He doesn't leave or yell at you when things get hard or messy. God isn't scared of your shortcomings. He covers them and shines light through them. He is always present and will never leave you or forsake you. That is a promise.

I encourage you to spend some time leaning into God as your whole and perfect Father. I wrote a devotional called, *Rise Up Princess* that speaks into who God is and what His promises are for you.

Our Heavenly Father is the only constant in our life, and He always will be if you let Him. Start by surrendering little things you worry about to God. See what happens.

1 Peter 5:7 commands us to cast all our cares on Him because He cares for us. Close your eyes and imagine yourself putting the situations you're worried about in a bag and throwing it up into Heaven. Imagine God catching it. You should feel the weight physically lift from your shoulders. Whether it is worrying about who you will marry, what school you will go to, which job you should take, paying off debt, or a medical report, you are royally invited to boldly present your requests at the throne and to peacefully wait for God's answer.

Try it: Present your requests to God, renew your mind, and continually remind yourself that you have access to the peace of God that transcends your understanding and will guard your mind and heart in the love of Jesus (Philippians 4:6–7).

> *Try it: Present your requests to God, renew your mind, and continually remind yourself that you have access to the peace of God that transcends your understanding and will guard your mind and heart in the love of Jesus.*

When you let go of the stress you aren't meant to carry, you'll have a peace in your heart that emanates through your eyes. You're His daughter, and it's time to start being and reflecting His peace.

Peace = The Sparkle Effect

Prayer

Dear Father:

I want to abide in You so You can abide in me. Please give me the discernment to know which things to cut out of my life that aren't bearing fruit and instead drain me. I declare I will begin to take hold of the fruit of peace that lives within me. Anxiety has no place in my mind, heart, or body. Worry is not a fruit of the Spirit and is not my inheritance.

Father, I want to be a faith girl. I want to fully, wholeheartedly believe You are who You say You are, and to believe in the promises You have for me. Let me live this life with the assurance that I don't have to worry because You love me so much, You'll care for me. Sometimes I feel like I'm carrying the weight of the world and I'm going to break down. But I am casting my troubles on You today; I surrender everything to You now in Jesus' name. When I pray and ask for things according to Your will, I will believe You can and are willing to answer me. I will not be double minded and doubt You.

I thank You that the Holy Spirit is my comforter and peace. As I grow in faith, I will lean more into You. Fill me with the supernatural rest and comfort that only comes from You. Guard my mind in Christ and make me firm and steadfast in faith. I will no longer be ruled by worry, but will be ruled by peace. I will enjoy the time between praying and being delivered. Amen.

Wonder Words

Peace I leave with you; my peace I give you. I do not give to you as the world gives. Do not let your hearts be troubled and do not be afraid.

—John 14:27

Do not be anxious about anything, but in every situation, by prayer and petition, with thanksgiving, present your requests to God. And the peace of God, which transcends all understanding, will guard your hearts and your minds in Christ Jesus.

—Philippians 4:6–7

"Come to me, all you who are weary and burdened, and I will give you rest. Take my yoke upon you and learn from me, for I am gentle and humble in heart, and you will find rest for your souls. For my yoke is easy and my burden is light."

—Matthew 11:28–30

Cast your cares on the LORD and he will sustain you; he will never let the righteous be shaken.

—Psalm 55:22

Afterword

I was in a conversation the other day and someone asked me, "If you could go back to any age in your life, what would it be and why?" I realized I wouldn't go back at all unless I could relive it all again with the freedom and wisdom I have now. I really hope this book unraveled years of my personal revelations for you so that you can emanate the radiance available to you now. I am the most fulfilled, secure, joyful, and content I have ever been. Not only am I thankful to essentially be living my dream life, I am filled with God's love. When circumstances aren't ideal and I am facing adversity, worry doesn't creep in like it used to. When the enemy uses people to accuse, gossip about, or reject me, it's certainly hurtful, but not devastating anymore. When I under-perform or let myself down, I don't spiral into depression. I can set boundaries and say "no" to something that doesn't honor God without fearing what someone will think. I can love others even when they don't love me. When someone asks me, "What do you do?" or "What have you been up to lately?" I don't feel the pressure to impress them.

When we are free of insecurity, depression, jealousy, fear, confusion, and people pleasing, the light of God can shine through our eyes. You can never be too broken for God to come in and restore you. As a matter of fact, it's the broken, stained glass where the most beautiful light glistens through. Whatever is meant for harm in your life, He will use for your good and His glory.

In Zechariah 9:16, God says He will save His people and they will sparkle in His land like jewels in a crown. You are made to sparkle. You are like a jewel in God's crown. This world needs you, your family needs you, your workplace needs you, and your school needs you. Our bleak world is desperate for women who sparkle and radiate with the security, confidence, and love of God. Your life, the light in your eyes, and the warmth in your presence are a letter to others about what real hope, identity, and purpose look like. You have the Sparkle Effect when your heart is touched by the Identity Transformer. You are adopted and married into the Royal Family.

You are:

A new creature

A bride

A princess

A friend

A servant

An heir

A saint

An ambassador

A being created for good works

A citizen of Heaven

A temple of God

A light

A city on a hill

A warrior

A royal priestess

A living stone

An alien and stranger to this world

A crown

A sparkle

Will you rise into your true identity? To be confidently set apart? Will you choose standards over settling? Will you let God transform you into the essence of who He made you to be? Step up, step out, and trust Him. Nothing will change until you do.

Your dream is waiting. The world is waiting. You are waiting. It's your time to stand out with a radiance beyond beauty. #TheSparkleEffect

Acknowledgments

I couldn't produce this book alone. I am so grateful to God for being so fun in giving me the vision for this book and then walking with me every step of the way. He's faithful to guide where He provides. He's transformed me from the inside out, which makes it so exciting to share my revelations with the hope to help others.

I wouldn't be the woman I am today without my husband, Kris. Thank you for continuously speaking life over me and standing so firm in reminding me of who I am in my moments of doubt. You are my biggest encourager. You edited my writings, talked through concepts, and sacrificed your own dreams for a time so I could pursue mine. You are a true man of strength and humility, and I am so blessed by you!

Kenzie, thank you for reading through every chapter. You were such a wonderful sounding board of wisdom and truth. Thank you for taking the time and interest to listen and love.

Julia, thank you for being my sparkle polisher. You call me out and present new viewpoints I may not have considered.

Mama and Daddy, I am so thankful you raised me with the knowledge and love for God. Thank you for exposing me to all of the opportunities you could and for propelling me on toward my biggest dreams. You shaped who I am, and I hope I will always make you proud.

To my agent, Margaret, thank you so much for reading my book and believing in it enough to take on my project. You effectively pitched and advocated for me through the whole process so we landed with my dream publisher!

To my women's group, y'all are the best cheerleaders ever! Thank you for calling out the gold, praying, interceding, sharing my excitement, and seeing God's dream for my life so clearly when I couldn't see it. You exemplify the power of women loving other women.

About the Author

Kristen Dalton Wolfe is a former Miss USA and the founder of SheIsMore.com, an inspirational online magazine that impacts more than 400,000 readers every month. She is a television host, personal coach, motivational speaker, and appears in global advertising campaigns. Kristen and her husband, Kris, live in Los Angeles with their daughter. Visit her website at SheIsMore.com.